When Government Doesn't Work Anymore

Perpetual Monopoly and the Loser's Paradox

What Happens When the Peasants Don't Want to Play?

Glenn A. Metts Ph.D.

Copyright © 2011 Pirate Publications
P O Box 307626
St Thomas, USVI 00803

Cover illustration by Gustavo Rodriguez
Interior illustrations by Rex May and Marty Bucella
Editing by Keith Aakre and Donna Urban

All rights reserved. No part of this publication may be reproduced, scanned, or distributed in any printed or electronic form without prior written permission of the publisher.

ISBN-13: 978-1467980920
ISBN-10: 1467980927

For additional information see www.peasantsociety.com

DEDICATION

I dedicate this book to the privileged and the peasants of the little blue planet; may we build a better world.

CONTENTS

	Acknowledgments	i
	Illustrations	iii
	Prologue	1
	Introduction	4
1	The Monopoly Game	14
2	The Perpetual Monopoly Game	28
3	Perpetual Monopoly And The Loser's Paradox	35
4	Perpetual Monopoly And The Winner's Paradox	40
5	The Importance Of Participation	49
6	So Let's Look At Some Interesting Numbers	66
7	Beyond *Perpetual* Monopoly To The Casino	84
8	Wealth, Corporate Influence, And Government Isolationism	106
9	Where Has All This Gotten Us?	116
10	What Are The Options?	128
11	The Solution To The Loser's Paradox	138
12	The Age Of Cooperation	145
	Appendix: Having Some Fun With Monopoly	150

ACKNOWLEDGMENTS

I want to acknowledge the contributions of the graveyard comic who had the wisdom to take advantage of a sad place to make me laugh.

ILLUSTRATIONS

Illustrations:

I.1	Variable rate social security…	6
1.1	The middle class…	17
4.1	Worked my way up to a king…	42
5.1	Go out and prosper…	52
7.1	Let them eat cake…	105
10.1	We all have to make sacrifices…	136

Figures:

6.1	Top one percent	76
6.2	Upward mobility	81
7.1	U.S. interest rate trends	102
8.1	The Wealth Cycle	107
9.1	Financial industry GDP share	126

Tables:

6.1	Comparison of Total Wealth and Total Investment in U.S. stock, bonds, and mutual funds in 2007	68
6.2	Percentage of total wealth held by US households in 2004	70
6.3	Three models of income distribution	72
6.4	Percentage of income taxes paid by different income groups	74
6.5	Income and Wealth Distribution Comparison	78

PROLOGUE

We are living in a time in America in which the very foundations of our society are shaken. From the halls of government to the board rooms of corporations, from the financial industry to Wall street and main street, there is an uneasiness about Our time. This time in our history is similar to the civil rights movement and the social anti-establishment upheaval of the nineteen-sixties; a time in our history in which change was forced on "unchangeable" forces. And like the sixties, eventually the unchangeable forces will have to capitulate and a new paradigm of economic thinking will emerge. We are at an inflection point that is demanding systemic change to our old economic model. Instead of race riots and demonstrations we will have economic riots and demonstrations. The demonstrations and riots will be global due to the inter-connectedness of social media and the fact that the under-lying economic issues that are the catalyst for unrest are also global.

Today we are witnessing the beginning of an economic uprising against the economic establishment and institutionalized wealth and privilege. In America the Monopoly[1] game is not fair anymore, it has produced institutionalized advantage and violated the very principles of our foundation, equality of opportunity and fairness. The economic uprising will once again challenge the greatness of America. The civil rights uprising of the sixties has been replaced by the economic uprising of the ten's with some notable differences. The number of people impacted by economic injustice is far greater, includes all races, both sexes, includes the vast majority of Americans, and has global participation.

There was a time not too long ago that saying some of the things here would have been unthinkable. Proposing it is time, perhaps, to leave Adam Smith to the history books and try to re-think our economic world is a radical change in the opinion of many American's responding to the state of humanity over the last decade. This thinking emerged from considering the unacceptable state of the human condition given all that we have at our disposal today and the profound inability of governments and current economic philosophies (and philosophers) to deal with those many citizens of the world that have become like the peasants of the feudal era. Considering the pervasive economic problems that have plagued Western economies over the last decade I realized more than ever that governmental and economic systems ultimately depend on the "peasants" to survive. The

---

[1] Reference to the Hasbro board game used as an analogy. Additional information available at http://www.hasbro.com/monopoly/en_US/

rulers and those in power need subjects, and when the subjects quit participating, the system breaks down. I also realized that my long held belief that it was those hard working capitalists, the entrepreneurs, and the producers of wealth that made everything work had a flaw. I realized that the flaw was that without participation of the masses, there is no sustainable government, economic activity, or "winners". That the capitalists, entrepreneurs, and producers of wealth are as dependent on the peasants as government is.

In an increasingly enlightened world nobody wants to be the peasant anymore, and come to think of it, why should they? Is it not possible for everybody to win, or at least a substantial majority? This is the challenge of our future economic system. The time has come for mankind to focus on mankind and realize that the state of humanity needs more attention. As citizens of that little blue planet we need to start looking at a new paradigm for an economic system that is up to the demands of a modern, inter-connected, inter-dependent global environment populated by more intelligent, capable, and enlightened humans than ever before.

Some will think this book is inciting instability with propaganda that predicts and points to the signs of our national demise. Some will think that I hate my own country and wish it would fail so that my criticisms could be justified. Some will think that I am a communist, or a socialist, anti-American, or anti-democratic, some may even think I am a patriot. You will have to decide for yourself.

INTRODUCTION

Today, it seems that governments, particularly the old democracies, just don't seem to work anymore. The age old institutions and economic models are failing us and no-one seems to know what to do about it. The economic controls and levers don't seem to produce the correct response and a national feeling of malaise has set in. Are we in Western democracies feeling the early signs of a system in decline, a system that is on the verge of collapse? I believe we are in a crisis that no-one, especially those institutionalized in the system, is willing to acknowledge much less sound an alarm. As our two parties blame each other and take turns fixing the proverbial mess left by the other party, the average American feels as if we are slipping away and no-body knows how to fix it. Our oldest democracies in Europe have faced one crisis after another as the media reports they are "muddling" through...... again. Not exactly sure what they mean by that word but it seems that is has something to do with "we really do not know how to fix this so we are going to do nothing and hope that it fixes itself"... yea something like that. What is happening in America? It seems as if we are going through one crisis after another as we follow the economic history of Europe's old democracies.

The "commies" are beating us at what was supposed to be "our" game. Our economic machine seems to be broken as we look to China now to buy our bonds and prop up our living standards by sending us cheap goods that even the unemployed can afford to buy,... thank you China, even our government likes this. I, like many Americans, thought it was the great democratic model that produced such vibrant economies, economic growth, and high standards of living. I thought the Chinese communists had brainwashed their young into believing they were doing the right thing and it was only a matter of time before they recognized the error of their ways and joined the "good guys".

Think about how the national view of China has been changing as we are bombarded with the success of their economic machine and huge trade surpluses that are the envy of the debt ridden West. They are looking better all the time as many of our citizens owe more on their homes than they are worth, have to deal with banks that can't or won't help them, have seen their retirement accounts cut in half by the sophisticated financial managers on wall street who took advantage of the last economic downturn to short the market into the dirt resulting in a tremendous wealth transfer from Americans retirement account to ????... oh we haven't found out who got the money yet. The raiding of the retirement accounts has delayed or destroyed the retirement of a generation, a generation whose golden years have become fool's gold for playing the Wall Street game. How will they retire and how will they live on retirement when the government is forced to reduce social security benefits in the future?

Illustration I.1

"It's an idea whose time has come! — Variable-Rate Social Security!"

Too many Americans feel that they are losing and the evidence clearly supports this notion. The growing wealth and income gap, the bail out of banks and Wall street but not main street, foreclosure of record numbers of homes, high unemployment, low interest rates on fixed income dependent citizens, unequal access to everything except food stamps and welfare, and the feeling that they are trapped in a system which they no longer support.

Our democracy has been compromised by corrupt politicians and political and legal processes that favor crony capitalism, influence peddling, and moral bankruptcy all for the mighty buck at the expense of the peasant citizens. Spending money we don't have by selling debt we can't re-pay to pay for graft, ineffective programs, and institutional benefits we can't afford. Government "by the people for the people" has become government "by the few for the few" and as government continues to grow it is no doubt going to be government "by the government for the benefit of government".

With the decline of good paying manufacturing jobs, the only good paying jobs left for the average citizen are those in government. A government that tells those who lost their jobs that they must be more competitive with cheap foreign labor or they must re-educate themselves at great expense to take low paying service jobs. A government that is itself not subjected to competition as it is comfortably isolated from global alternatives. A government that is bloated, inefficient, and dysfunctional in every respect. Is this Our democracy?

I remember being a freshman in college and my professor talking about the "command" economies of socialist countries such as the U.S.S.R. and China. They "controlled" their economies with five-year plans and did not allow the free flow of self-correcting economic activity. Now we hear American TV commentators speaking of the success of China, pointing to the five-year plans as a positive thing (CNBC guest in October 2011). "They actually plan" they said……thought planning was a no-no that interfered with the natural forces of a market economy, remember, "just stay out of the way and it will fix itself"…….really? Apparently this lazier-faire attitude blacked out when the big banks were bailed out.

In the "West" we followed the prodigious Adam Smith and subsequent economic modifications of a system destined to become the future economic model of the world,….. it was only a matter of time before Western civilizations saved the world from their foolish economic propositions. This seemed to be true for a very long time – but today we have begun to doubt it more than just a bit as many citizens of the world who live in the Western economies, are feeling the paralyzing malaise that has long set in throughout many parts of Europe.

So what is the problem? Or better yet…. what is the solution? Have we like many past great civilizations suddenly become incapable of making our system work? What happened to those Romans anyway? Was it malaise that took them down? Was it the fact that Roman citizens lost interest in their own civilization? We know that the armies of the later Roman Empire largely consisted of non-Romans… was that the problem…. or a sign of the problem? We can be sure that the Roman resistance to those invading Barbarians was not up to par with the Rome of old, they just didn't have the fight in them anymore. Did the average citizen in Rome care? Did they think that they probably wouldn't be worse off under the Barbarians? Did they think that since the Roman government had taken care of them for so long that they were just getting a new caretaker? Of course we have argued about all of this for millennia and have not found an undisputable answer, nor will we here.

What the hell let's give it a try……… I propose that more than anything else it was ultimately the lack of participation of the Roman citizen that produced the factors critical to the fall. By the time the barbarians were invading Rome not only were there virtually no Roman citizens serving in the military, but the average Roman citizen had checked out of the system. They reached a tipping point in which the masses did not see the invading Barbarians as being any worse than the corrupt Roman heads of state and the untouchable classes of wealth that had limited the real opportunities of the lower classes for centuries, in other words the citizens themselves took Rome down. Their lack of desire to defend her and their lack of faith in their future under her thumb produced a citizenry that had become indifferent to her survival. The invading Barbarians at a minimum promised a change that would undo the failed system that had not taken care of her citizens…..our government politicians might be surprised at the number of Americans who would welcome such radical change.

It is interesting however, to think about the inability of civilizations to survive when the heartbeat of their citizens slows to a patter. The agnostics are most unhappy with "In God We Trust" on our currency but when you think about the concept of faith, and its' role in the sustainability of any governmental system, we have to consider what happens when people just do not "believe" anymore. Faith in your government and believing in your system is vitally important and I would assume that without these things any governmental system will fail. Therefore we all must concede that the role of faith in governmental systems is important, even if it is not in God. Likewise confidence is important, if not critical for the same reason. As we see one politician after another try to inspire us out of our national malaise I am beginning to think that they get it too.

The economists have understood this role for a long period of time as they point to negative consumer confidence as the cause of economic downturns and a positive change in that confidence as the way out. Maybe we need to come up with a mind altering drug that will cause us all to be irrationally confident so that we can live in economic nirvana forever. The Chemtrail people may have already discovered the solution. Maybe you haven't heard but the government, according to this kooky group, has been spraying us for years. The theory is that the jets trails in the sky are really a chemical bomb that is being spewed on all of us in a massive depopulation effort. Can you think of a better way to control the peasants? Perhaps the government could use mind altering drugs instead to trick us all into thinking that the government is great so we will behave. Come to think of it.... maybe this group is not so kooky after all.

Throughout 2010 and 2011 we witnessed the Fed incrementally applying one tool after another to try to get things moving again, but nothing seemed to really work effectively. We fixed the banks, we fixed the big corporations that were going bankrupt, and now all we need to do is make wall street happy and we will all be eating apple pie again and singing kumbaya. Many experts think that all this economic manipulation is either critical to recovery (the Keynesians) or destroying the system (the supply siders). What is that again?..... trickle up.... trickle down.....how bout trickle in my pocket..... most of us really do not care how it gets there. Actually, most Americans do not care who is right on this, they just want to be able to make their lives work and preserve something for future generations. Regardless of which side the economist is on we are to either tweak the system or leave it alone completely...... remember laissez-faire?

Is this working? I think one of the most challenging problems we face is the fact that we now live in a global community that is inter-connected like never before in history. If you think about it, corporations are global, financial systems span the globe, BUT governments do not. Are national governments, which are limited by their borders, able to control a global financial system and corporate environment? Could this be part of the problem?

As we have moved from villages, to towns, to regions, and nations we have watched the governmental and economic systems change. We are now in a global system with an economic system designed for nations. Will our old economic ideas work? Do we need to rethink our economic model? We are at a point in time in which our economic system and theories are perhaps outdated and a new paradigm is needed. Perhaps we need to think radically, not incrementally. Have we reached the end of our ability to incrementalize ourselves out of it? Are we incrementalizing ourselves into oblivion?

The natural tendency of mankind is to make incremental improvements to institutions and economic systems. As we stand in fear of dramatic change we attempt to make small changes to a system over a long period of time as a way of dealing with uncertainty. This tendency makes perfect sense given that it works most of the time, however, there have been inflection points in history which have demonstrated that incrementalism ultimately does not work and leads to failure. These are times in which we need to re-think our economic institutions and governmental systems and open our mind to dramatic change. Otherwise, the malaise of the masses may ultimately take down the whole system, not necessarily through revolution but simply by refusing to participate.

We watch on TV as the unrest unfolds around the world – modern mankind has lost faith in the system's ability to improve their lives. Whether it is the street demonstration in London, Wall Street in New York, or in Italy, Greece and on and on… we see a modern movement that is informed, connected, aided by technology that is sending a strong message that the gig is up, we need something different.

Players in our system have largely been educated in a system that is showing signs of failure world-wide. Is capitalism the answer anymore? As we move into the future, this assertion, which is largely defended by those who have benefited from it most, will be challenged like never before. Is mankind's need for government changed? Has modern mankind's intelligence finally super-ceded the shadow-box of political demagoguery? Has "The Wealth of Nations"[2] run into the global community? We live in a global environment that is multi-lingual, multi-cultural, inter-dependent, and connected through technology like never before in history of mankind.

Whatever happens, "The Wealth of Nations" is not working for far too many, and it is better to transition out of our current system than to wait for the alternative which may be chaos driven by collapse. Embrace a new paradigm before we incrementalize

---

[2] Reference to Industrial Capitalism based on the work of Adam Smith whose book "An Inquiry into the Nature and Causes of the Wealth of Nations" (shortened to "The Wealth of Nations") in 1776 became the basis for capitalism in America.

ourselves into oblivion. We have a good chance of doing this in a very positive way by turning some of our energy and our best minds to the task of re-imagining an economic system built for a global community. One of the obstacles in such a transition is our ability to convince those who have benefited most from our current system, including our national governmental systems, to allow new thinking to emerge. The ability of those on the verge of experiencing what I call the Winner's Paradox to understand that sustainability is only possible when those experiencing the Loser's Paradox can believe once again that they can also win, have hope, and have a brighter future.

1

THE MONOPOLY GAME

I remember walking through a graveyard when I was much younger and seeing a headstone that read "Help! I Can't Breathe". I immediately laughed and felt amused and somehow connected to the person buried under that headstone and wished I had known them when they were alive. A person who even in death, was making strangers laugh in a cemetery, many of whom would be there on a sad occasion. There was a message in those few words to everyone who happened to walk by - that humor and laughter were somehow important enough even to be considered after death. You have to admire the forethought of a person who would make such a decision, a decision to use the small space of a headstone not to tell me about their accomplishments but to make me laugh.

As I began this book writing project I felt that the headstone inscription reflected our situation in America today, it seems we are having trouble breathing, and laughing. Many Americans are feeling less hopeful, less well off, and less American than perhaps at any time in our history save the great depression. Too many of our citizens are having trouble breathing and no-one seems to know how to fix it. It seems that government doesn't work anymore, our economic system is broken, and the future is just a shadow of the past. There is a malaise that is infecting us and like the sadness in the graveyard, we also need to laugh.

In this book I hope to contribute some humor, encouragement and a serious discussion about the future of economic systems and humanity. Our little blue planet is getting really small and we are all connected in ways we never were before. The little blue planet is just going to feel smaller in the future. We need to find better ways to get along and better ways for all of humanity to experience the benefits of our age. We live in a time of marvelous advances in technology, medicine, education, science, and knowledge. Unfortunately our social and economic systems have not kept up with our advances in other areas. With knowledge doubling every few years, the pace of our progress on one of the most important influences in our lives, our economic and governmental systems, seem by comparison old, out of date, and draconian when compared to the speed of change in the rest of our world. It is time we start closing this gap, it is time we consider some new approaches to managing the governmental and economic systems that support us, the ones that really can make us laugh or can make us gasp for air. We have to stop thinking of them as a historical monument that is immune to change and further development to respond to a changing world. Our governmental and economic systems should keep pace with humanity. It is time we stop incrementally tweaking the old car and consider getting a new one. We may be incrementalize ourselves into oblivion as valuable time is spent trying to keep the establishment established.

We also need to think beyond our borders since the age of nations is passing quickly before us never to be seen again. Our problems are not just in America, they have gone global along with our technology, our large corporations and financial systems. Many people on the little blue planet are having a peasant experience rather than a pleasant experience as they struggle to get by in our modern world. Many feel like the homeless window shopper at Christmas time, they see and understand the opportunity for a better life but somehow it just seems to be out of reach.

Many people in Western democracies today are feeling like they are losing the battle for a better life. Even those who have played by the rules are not able to win. The Monopoly game is not going very well as they seem to be losing every game. Their lives are like a silent movie as they have no voice in a system that seems to be run by and designed for the few, not the many. We are in a modern day version of the feudal era, a time of great advantage for a few and the powerlessness of the masses. The winners in America today are winning on a grand scale and too many of the modern day peasants are losing. We are losing our middle class and are beginning to look more like the anti-democracies that we were not. We need to find a way for more of us to win, even most of us.

We should not be discouraged by the fact that humanity has never been able to design such a system of government and economics. After all, it was not that long ago that we were without the computers and other electronic devices that have connected the world in an amazingly short period of time. Our progress in economic and governmental systems is dismal by comparison. Surely we can we do better than this, surely we can find more shoes for the peasants.

Illustration 1.1

"...And the ones wearing shoes are the *middle class*."

Throughout this book I use the Monopoly game to illustrate and tinker with our economic thinking. In this chapter we will review the basics of old Monopoly to lay the ground work for the perpetual Monopoly game presented in the next chapter. We are going to look at two natural outcomes of the Monopoly game, what I call the Loser's Paradox and the Winner's Paradox. We will use these two concepts to help connect the perpetual Monopoly game to our real economic lives and to illustrate the nature of our true interdependence. The later chapters will add more information about some of the things that are not going to well in America and we will conclude with some observations about the future.

Not very many people get too excited about reading a book on government and economics or even participating in the discussion. While we are all impacted by the economy it seems overly complicated and beyond our ability to change. This simply is not so, we do still vote in America, for a while longer anyway, and if enough Americans want change they still get it. The fact that economics can be boring is why I chose to write about Monopoly instead, most Westerners can identify with the game because of its popularity over the last four or five generations. Besides, this book really isn't about economics and government anyway, it is simply about living.

The history of Monopoly is as amazing as the current financial entanglements in Western economies. There will be no attempt to re-state it here with the exception of this short commentary. If you are interested in a rather exhaustive explanation I encouraged you to access Wikipedia[3] or one of several

---

[3] Wikipedia, on the history of the Monopoly game, http://en.wikipedia.org/wiki/history_of_the_board_game_Monopoly, (October 2011).

other links covering the history of the game. Monopoly dates back to early versions produced in 1903. The popular game today is the product of many modifications that resulted in the version presented by Charles Darrow to Parker Brothers who began marketing the game in 1935. Although there is significant history of the game prior to the first Parker Brothers version, Parker Brothers does not recognize any of the games' history prior to Charles Darrow for rather obvious reasons, they purchased the game rights from Charles.

The game is a simple example of an economic system and it has many of the same components that we find in our modern Western economies. Each player moves around a square board with the role of dice and they buy land, pay some bills, hopefully manage their money, play responsibly, and have a little bit of good luck. All these things are necessary to win. And winning can be quite exhilarating since you may have to play for hours, depending on the rules you use, to actually finish the game. There have been world championships played for decades and people connect to the game in the Western economies because it is a primer of sorts for the economic system that we have had in place for a few hundred years. Today there are on-line games and various versions to capture a wider international market. Playing the game is so simple that a 10 year old can understand the game well enough to play.

When you first play the game you are unskilled and you really do not know the rules very well. You will most likely lose at this game early on, but that's OK since you are "just a beginner". Over time you get better at the game and finally you experience nirvana with your first win. As most of us already know, we win at Monopoly when everybody else goes broke. Awesome experience winning is, and in life, like in Monopoly, some people experience this more than others. For some, it may start with the Monopoly game itself. You know who I am talking about here, that friend or family member who seems to be unusually good at Monopoly, a person who seems to have the right combination of luck and skill and just seems to always win. The consequence of winning all the time is that those who have lost too many times do not want to play the game anymore, at least with them.

So let us review the rules of the old Monopoly game that we love so dearly before we move on. Each player is given a certain amount of money from the bank, and play begins as we roll the dice and begin our move around the board. If we are lucky enough with the dice we can land on a piece of property that we can buy, provided we have the money to pay for it, we can also land on a penalty spot, or community chest or chance. Landing on Community Chest or Chance we draw a card that may benefit us or make us pay a penalty. And we all know that every time we pass "GO" we collect $200 from the bank, this is the original government handout. You can also buy and improve property like a slum lord or Donald Trump depending on your skill and luck. There are so many parallels between the game and real life that we should discuss some of them here.

The board

The board represents your life, at least your economic life. It presents you with risks and opportunities based on your ability to manage your money and spend it wisely, avoid pitfalls that involve penalties, and make good economic decisions. The board includes different types of properties such as land, utilities, and railroads. The properties are arranged from the lowest cost pieces at the beginning of your trip around the game board to more expensive options as you move clockwise around the board. The trip around the board has many subtle connections to real life. For one, the properties are grouped according to cost much like our real life neighborhoods in which similar cost housing is found lumped together. As we move around the board the options become more expensive which is similar to real life in the sense that we typically consider "moving up" and buying more expensive properties as we go through life.

The money

The money we receive at the beginning of the game represents our inheritance. This inheritance comes to us in many forms. We have biological factors, environmental factors from our upbringing, and money inheritance if we are lucky. Biological factors we inherit can help us be successful according to research that shows relationships between intellect, physical characteristics and economic success in life. Environmental factors from our upbringing include our learning exposure and other experiences generally provided by our home environment but also include experiences outside the home. In life things that happen to us while we are growing up can have a tremendous impact on our economic lives. A teacher that took interest in you, a friend's parent that served as a particularly good role model, that aunt who intentionally lost to us in checkers so we could experience winning, or a mentor in a job or career path all can make a huge difference.

<u>The dice</u>
The dice represents the fact that luck and good fortune play an important role in our economic lives. A lucky role of the dice can put you on a desirable piece of land that no-one has purchased and therefore provide you with a valuable opportunity. Another lucky role of the dice can cause you to avoid landing on an opponent's piece of property that is stacked with hotels or houses which can drain your financial resources from paying rent. Both the financial opportunities and the financial pitfalls depend on the role of the dice. Of course having an opportunity and being in a position to take advantage of it often requires resources, just like in real life. So landing on that nice piece of property does not mean we can buy it. And just like in real life, a streak of bad luck in Monopoly can cause you to lose even if you have done everything else very well. This is ultimately the equalizer between age groups playing the game.

While age gives you better skills and experience, these can be neutralized by bad luck. Community Chest and Chance represent the breaks, good and bad, that life throws at us, events we have to adjust to in order to keep playing. We can win money, have to pay a fine, draw a "get out of jail free" card (Bernie Madoff needed one of these) or be thrown in jail, all at the roll of the dice. Just like in real life things happen along the way that are completely unknown until they happen, such events are represented by the Community Chest and Chance cards.

When Government Doesn't Work Anymore

Respect for age and experience

Passing Go and getting $200 represents the reward for surviving the game of life to a certain age and gaining certain rights, privileges, and benefits from surviving. We are rewarded in real life for the "passage of time" privileges like driving a car, choosing whether or not we wanted to continue with our education, moving out of our parent's house, decide what we want to do for a living and where we want to live. Survival has important benefits in every culture and other cultures are no different even though the markings of progress are often different. The alternate way to view the $200 you receive for passing go has already been mentioned; a government handout. A government handout can be a valuable economic benefit at the right time. Many of our government handout programs have provided important help at a critical time, unfortunately not all government handouts have equal usefulness in the real economy.

Taxes and the role of government

Perhaps the most curious thing about the Monopoly game is the role of government. Whether or not you pay any taxes at all is completely dependent upon the unlucky role of the dice that lands you on the tax square. How cool would this be in real-life? It makes you wonder where we went wrong here, how about we roll the dice at the end of each year and see if we have to file taxes for the past year. Don't think the government would ever agree to this. In Monopoly, even if you have to pay taxes, the rate in the traditional game is either a $200 estimate or 10% of all your assets. These are rates we could live with today but actually have no connection to the actual rates in 1935; believe it or not tax rates in 1935 were much higher than the Monopoly game indicates. Few people paid income taxes in 1935 and lower income levels paid virtually none but the highest income tax rate in 1935 was 63% (for one million and more in income) and the capital gains tax (tax on stock gains for instance) was 31.5%. If you ignore the rates themselves we can read some additional insight into the minimum rate of $200 which you have to pay even if you have only $200. This is contrary to modern income tax policy which essentially taxes the bottom 50% of payers nothing but collects significant other-than-income taxes in the form of social security, Medicare, sales, excise, and several other taxes that are built into products and services that we all must purchase to live in our modern world..... no real tax break after all. Unlike the real world, Monopoly does not include any relationship between taxes that you pay and income. We might forgive this defect given the fact that the boom in the Monopoly game that began in 1935 was at a time in which a significant number of people had very low incomes anyway.

The bank

The bank in the Monopoly game is another curious component. You have to admire what the official rules say about the Bank, the direct quote is

> "The Bank never goes broke. If the Bank runs out of money, the Banker may issue as much more as may be needed by writing on any ordinary paper"[4].

---

[4] Official Monopoly game rules from Hasbro available at http://www.hasbro.com/common/instruct/monins.pdf, (October 2011).

Maybe this is what those congressmen and women were reading when they bailed them out, could it be so? As most of us know we get to choose among ourselves the person we want to be the banker in the game, basically the only requirement is that they can count and make change. The bank in Monopoly is similar to the modern day credit union. The bank is also a surrogate for the government in that the bank technically owns all the property at the beginning of the game and receives the money when a property is sold. In America a considerable amount of unclaimed land is considered owned by the government and even though we the tax payer may have paid for it once (i.e. Louisiana Purchase) we paid again to buy it from the government. This by the way is the result of a sense of fairness that most people possess; why shouldn't' they pay the "tax payers" back?, a concept that often eludes our modern day government.

The bank does not loan money, is the chief real estate broker, and auctioneer, another concession to simplify the game. Even with the shortcut at the bank and quirky tax policy the game by and large represents the major components of our financial lives and many people feel that if they win at Monopoly it means something. It may mean that they have the ability to be successful in the real world since they have demonstrated some skills that are still critically important today.

Winning the game

Ultimately, someone wins the game when everyone else is broke, kind of an extreme form of capitalism. The person that has exhibited the best combination of skill and luck wins; the only thing missing from our real economy is privilege. You have to manage your money, make good decisions, and of course be lucky, kind of like real life. It seems inherently fair overall since we all started out the game with the same opportunities, the same amount of money from the bank, used the same dice, and had been given our turns to roll the dice. At the end of the game we can have a number of reactions from the players based on their individual experiences playing the game.

Assuming that we had four players in the game let's go through each player's emotions and feelings hypothetically after the game has ended. The winner is feeling pretty good as they now have all the money and probably most if not all the property and the satisfaction that they are now king of the Monopoly world. The nirvana of winning is kind of a happy/sad moment though since the winner realizes at the moment of victory there is no one else to play with, the game is over, and they are really not going to be able to take the time to enjoy their fabulous victory by freely moving about the board unaffected by the hazards that others would face such as the hotels on Park Place and the Tax square that seems more onerous on the poorer players with less cash.

The person who finished second in the game is not feeling too bad either. They almost beat everybody and coming in second place makes them feel that they can win next time, after all, they came so close. The second place person is probably the person in the game that is ready to play again immediately because the taste of victory was almost in their grasp. In a similar way the third place person is consoled by the fact that, while they did not win, at least they did not come in last. This person may feel somewhat hopeful in their ability to win eventually, they may think they just need more practice playing the game. This person is probably not ready to play again immediately, but the game has not left any lingering bitter taste in their mouth.

The person who finished last is the real loser. While there was only one winner based on the game rules and everyone else lost, this person knows that some people lose worse than others. Being the first person out in the Monopoly game makes you the biggest loser and leaves this individual with some serious doubt about their skills and abilities as it relates to the game. Just like in real life, this person, somewhat depending on age, realizes that no-one loses all the time in real life and is willing to play the game again but not anytime soon, they first have to figure out a different approach to the game. They know down deep that losing was not just a result of bad luck, down deep they feel that they are not very good at the skills necessary to win. Given some time maybe they can become better at Monopoly as they gain more experience. If this person is the youngest of the players they may also be consoled by the feeling that they "were supposed to lose" because of their youth.

2

THE *PERPETUAL* MONOPOLY GAME

$\mathcal{E}$veryone who has spent some time playing Monopoly realizes that the game diverges from real life in many ways. We covered a few of these in the prior chapter but there are more differences we need to explore. Our first additional observation will be that in real life, when someone wins, the game does not end like in Monopoly. In the last chapter we talked about the winner having a bitter/sweet experience because at their moment of nirvana they suddenly realize that they really will not be able to enjoy their win, or for that matter their winnings, for very long. The game ends leaving them unable to enjoy the extreme wealth and advantage that they have gained. A second observation is that in real life we have many winners, or so it seems, and so we do not just have "a" winner, we have an entire group of them. This can be quite inspiring since the more people we see win, the more we feel like our day may be just over the horizon, we can win too. Our final observation is that the real life game is perpetual, it does not stop, is never reset, and just goes on and on, in reality it is a perpetual Monopoly game.

<u>Expand the money supply</u>

So now let's imagine a perpetual Monopoly game that does not have an end. In order to have a perpetual game we are definitely going to have to alter the rules a bit for this to work, so let us consider some of these here. One of the first things we see is that in order for the perpetual Monopoly game to work we would need to print more money not just scraps of paper that represent more money since the game only has a limited amount of money. How are we going pay everyone to pass "GO" if the bank runs out of money? Therefore we have new rule number one; the government/bank has the authority to print more money.

<u>Create a government</u>

This brings up a good point – should the bank continue to be a proxy for the government? I don't think so. We are going to have to fix this too. Let's see, maybe we could create a separate government by having the player's pick someone or some group of player's to be the government. The government will then be able to collect monies off the income tax square, and of course, the government will still keep all their money in the bank. Maybe we could have the government watch the banker, since we're not sure we will trust the banker, especially after a few generations of perpetual Monopoly. Therefore new rule number two is that the perpetual Monopoly government will be elected from the players. When a player dies they are automatically removed from the government and a new player is elected to take their place.

<u>Inheritance</u>

Oh my, another problem has become way to obvious, in a perpetual Monopoly game the player's will die before the game ends. We definitely have to do something about this or our goal of making the game perpetual is sure to fail. There may be several ways to address this problem, but one thing is certain, the game cannot go on if no-one is playing it. One possibility is to have the government get all the money and property of the dead player and give it to some poor players. Another idea is that we could have the government only get part of the dead players money and property and have the rest of it passed on to their children or poor players. And of course a third option would be to have all the money and property just go to the children without the government getting anything. If we have the player pass their money and property onto their children it's kind of like the dead player is still in the game.

There is something nice about that, besides, why should anyone else benefit from their hard work? Being that we are just imagining this game we better keep things simple so new rule number three is that all property and money of a dead player will pass to their children, I am sure the children will like this rule, especially if they have not had much luck playing the game. Of course we are going to have to think of something to help all those children whose parents did not have such a good run at the game and don't have anything to pass on, I mean, how fair is that? –

shouldn't everyone get an even start just like the regular Monopoly game?

Making the game mandatory

Now that I am into this perpetual Monopoly thing I am beginning to realize that we run the risk of some player actually quitting the game. Losing is one thing but quitting is something different altogether. As the old saying goes, "for every winner there is a loser"…..well maybe more than one loser. We need to keep the losers playing the game, otherwise we will have no definition of winning. I mean how can you win if there are no losers to compare yourself to? Come to think of it though, I guess you can quit in the regular Monopoly game, but what if everybody quits?, or what if so many people quit that there are not enough people left to play the game? Humph, this could be the ultimate risk in perpetual Monopoly, we better make it mandatory to play the game, otherwise - How can we be certain that it will continue?, we certainly do not want anybody starting another game, otherwise we will have competing games and that may put the perpetual Monopoly game out of business and once again, the whole idea of the game being perpetual will fail.

Expansion of the board

Since population seems to increase over-time and everybody has to play the game we need to address the limitations of the board. Think about it, if we are going to have an increasing number of people playing this game we need to make some accommodations. Probably the best way to do this is to figure out how to make the board larger and a little more interesting. Probably the best way to do this is give the bank/government the authority to expand the board along with the amount of printed money in the game. Geographically speaking we could enlarge the board by invading another game and taking over their board or we could take the peaceful approach and just sub-divide the current board into smaller parcels, kind of like making Board Walk into lower Manhattan or something like that. If we did this there would be enough property to go around, even if we had to stack the houses vertically to make it work. Along this same vein we need to allow players to buy and sell properties more than once, otherwise the game will become boring and no-body will want to play anymore.

Ok, I think we have done a fair job of making some rule changes. I think we only need one more..... you know what I am thinking about don't you? We need a rule about making rules. We may find out along the way that we made a mistake in rule making and really need to change the rules a bit to make sure the game remains perpetual. We have a couple of problems here...., I mean, understanding why you might need to change the rules is easy enough for everybody to understand, but who should have the authority to make new rules.

In the old Monopoly game we didn't have to think about this at all, the rules just came with the game. Besides, in the old game if you really didn't like the rules you just didn't play the game. But in perpetual Monopoly everybody has to play and therefore we have to make sure that the rules are fair.... or... at least we have to make sure that everyone thinks the rules are fair. So who do we give this power to? Well we could give it to the bank, but then, who is the banker anyway? – oh no – another problem, we can't just let anybody have the bank –how are we going to do this? I guess we are not done with the rules yet. Let's think now… the bank…, we need a way of selecting the banker that will be fair. In Monopoly you really need to trust the banker, and in perpetual Monopoly we may be dealing with this banker a long time, especially given new rule number three…. they could pass it on to their children.

Should the government choose the banker? After all, we are selecting the government from all the players, so isn't that like representative banking or something? That's it! the government can choose the banker that way if the players don't like the banker they can complain to the government, who is elected by the players, who because they know they have to play the game forever will surely demand that any banker that does not do the job honorably will have to quit being the banker.

Almost forgot what we were doing here, now we have to go back to the rule about rule making. As I said before, since the perpetual Monopoly game is…. well….. perpetual, we may need to tune up these rules from time to time so we definitely need the rule of rules. We need to make sure this process is responsive to the majority of players so we can keep everybody as happy as possible and make timely updates to the perpetual Monopoly rules. Once again, the obvious choice is the government for the same reason as it is for the banking problem. You know, I am beginning to think that the government is playing too big a role in this new game, every time we need to make a decision or in this case a new rule, we keep putting it on the government.

This brings up another question here, how big does this government need to be? Think about it, if the government gets to big we are going to have to make some really unpopular changes to the income tax square.

3

PERPETUAL MONOPOLY AND THE LOSER'S PARADOX

Let us imagine playing our imaginary game. It is easy to see that over time some players will have managed to gain control over the most valuable properties, built them up with houses and hotels, and managed to have most of the money. With such advantage it is hard to imagine how they could ever lose the game except for some extended period of extremely poor judgment or very bad luck. As these winners pass the game on to the newer family members we end up with generations that inherit the advantages of past successes. These past successes of their forbearers may help insulate them from the normal struggles of life and the potential failures that one faces without such advantage.

For those who are not winning the game, a grim reality sets in. It seems that no matter how much effort they make, and no matter how well they know the rules, it seems that they just cannot win. These players start looking for a way to change the game or at least quit since they feel that playing a game one cannot ever win is a waste of time. They feel they either have to improve their chances of winning by changing the rules or they will just quit participating altogether. The problem for them is that if they quit there is surely no chance of them ever winning. These players start experiencing what I call the Loser's Paradox.

The Loser's Paradox

The Loser's Paradox is experienced in three different phases by a player in a game. The first phase of the Loser's Paradox is when a player has consistently lost at a game to the point that they do not want to play anymore. At this point the player may view their reasons for failure as internal or external. If they believe they are either not good enough or not lucky enough to ever win they internalize their loss and they do not blame the game itself. If on the other hand they believe that the game itself is somehow unfair or the rules are stacked in the winners favor they externalize the loss. Externalizing the loss is a much more dangerous view since blaming the game or the rules will make them want to change either or both and that can be destabilizing to the game.

The second phase of the Loser's Paradox is when a player decides to quit the game. This is hard since quitting is a second loss in the sense that they are not only losing but admitting that they have lost. Quitting is demoralizing and is never without consequences to confidence, an important ingredient in winning. Wait a minute they can't quit, we made a rule about that. If they can't quit they will probably just sat there and not participate…you know….they will just roll the dice, move around the board, not do anything like purchase property and run out of money and…..then what? What are we going to do when they run out of money? If they MUST play we are going to have to give them some money to keep them in the game. I guess the government can borrow some money from the bank and loan it to them. I can see a problem here with this game, if a lot of players quit participating it is going to cost a lot of money. It's a good thing we made the rule about creating money.

The final phase of the Loser's Paradox is realizing that the only way for them to ever win is to play the game. Herein lies the paradox, the very solution to the loser's problem is to play the game and win, an option that they will have passed over if they quit or stop participating in the game.

<u>Implications of the Loser's Paradox</u>

We can summarize the Loser's Paradox up as the balance between the desire not to continue losing with the desire to win. The necessary condition for increasing the desire to win for a person who has been losing excessively is that the person must believe that their opportunity to win has improved. That it has changed in some significant way from when they were losing excessively. Therefore for the loser to be willing to continue playing there has to be some moderation in the game conditions that entices them to play.

The basic conditions of the Loser's Paradox are summed up in the following statements.

When a player has lost excessively, their desire not to lose is greater than their belief that they can win so they do not play the game.

Desire not to lose > Belief that they can win   does not play

When a players desire not to lose is equal to their belief they can win they are indifferent toward playing the game.

Desire not to lose = Belief that they can win   indifferent to play

When a players desire not to lose is less than their belief they can win they are going to resume playing the game

Desire not to lose < Belief that they can win   play resumes

The implication of this in any economic relationship is that the belief that one can win is a precondition for a player's participation. It is easy to understand how a player's belief that they can win would decline when they have lost excessively. The important thing to consider then is what can change this belief enough to make them want to play again. Such a change in the player's belief about winning is either going to come from within the player (internal) such as a change in confidence from additional experience or externally such as a change to the conditions surrounding the game such as a change in the rules in their favor. If the losing player has enough influence over the rules of the game, they may try to change the rules to make the game "more fair" in their perception. If they do not have such influence they are likely to choose not to play until someone with such power changes the game for them.

Back to the aunt who intentionally lost to us in checkers mentioned in Chapter 1. The aunt had an obvious advantage over the child so the aunt could consistently win at checkers. Knowing that winning all the time would cause the child to not want to play since it would demoralize the child, the aunt chose not to apply all her skills and let the child win. The aunt did this because she thought that winning was good for the child, in fact, she thought that winning was more important for the child than it was for herself. The child's confidence increased and with the increase in confidence the child kept playing, obtained better skills, and eventually gave the aunt a good game. In order for the child's belief to change, the aunt had to cooperate. In other words, the key to changing the child's belief about his/her ability to win was the aunt's willingness to help the child.

In the perpetual Monopoly game, like any economic system, the survival of the game relies on participation. Lack of participation causes collapse. If enough individuals quit participating in our economy it will collapse. The same is true for the tax system, the stock market, the banking system, even our government. Our entire economic system in America is dependent on participation. So the implication of the Loser's Paradox is that if enough players do not believe they can win and quit participating, their lack of participation will cause the system to collapse.

4

PERPETUAL MONOPOLY AND THE WINNER'S PARADOX

It is such a drag talking about all this losing stuff... What about winning, don't we all want to win? Let's talk about winning for a while, after all, what happens to the winners in perpetual Monopoly? If we are a winner we are indeed a little happier than the loser, especially in perpetual Monopoly. Rather than have the game start over with a level playing field we are able to enjoy our success indefinitely, once we have gained an advantage….. or are we?

It seems that once we have the upper hand we can, and should, work at preserving our success. It is our duty to our heirs and besides, it is simply not American to play less hard just because you have an advantage. What person wants to win that game of checkers with their aunt because she really didn't play her best? We knew it all along and it robbed us of our true feeling of victory. What was our aunt thinking anyway, did she think she was helping us or something? Did she think that is the only way we could win? Why did our aunt do that?….. Did she know something that we didn't know?

Back to perpetual Monopoly………..

We all like to win and the longer the winning streak the better, that is why there are so few examples of individuals forsaking their material possessions in favor of a better life. I think the last person to do that was a member of the Borden dairy family and heir to the Borden, Inc. family fortune in the early 1900's. William Whiting Borden[5] became a missionary and died in training in Egypt in 1913….. so much for a better life.

In perpetual Monopoly the winning players become institutionalized at winning. By this statement I mean that if you are winning in perpetual Monopoly you have an advantage over other players which makes it easier to keep on winning. This is like some natural law that we see in many aspects of life, it is like what we have done in the past accrues to our benefit in the future. None of us really see anything wrong with this idea in the sense that we think it fair enough for someone's hard work to payoff. The problem with institutionalized winning is that this statement becomes less true as the winning baton is passed to future generations.

Suddenly their systematic right to assuming the position of their forbearers is challenged by current players who do not have such privilege. A similar reaction occurs if we think our ability to win is

---

[5] Wikipedia, William Whiting Borden, http://en.wikipedia.org/wiki/ William_ Whiting_Borden , (October 2011).

hampered, not by our own lack of effort and playing by the rules, but instead is hampered by a system that has two sets of rules; one for the winners and one for the losers. Nobody minds losing as much if they really believe that the game is fair even if they have to start at the bottom.

Illustration 4.1

"You can do anything if you just put your mind to it. Look at me. I had to start out as a Prince and work my way up to King."

Ultimately there is a problem with winning in the perpetual Monopoly game, something I refer to as the Winner's Paradox. The Winner's Paradox stems from the fact that winning continuously or excessively causes problems in the system. So let us imagine how this can happen.

The Winner's Paradox

In perpetual Monopoly, being able to transfer property and money from one generation to the next gives subsequent generations the upper hand in the game. After several generations of winners, the odds of losing decrease significantly and the perception that the game is fair becomes a problem. Those who are losing on a regular basis quit participating and this begins to affect the winners. Just like the card shark, the perpetual winner has a problem convincing the losers to hang in there.

Phase one of the Winner's Paradox is winning excessively. Such excessive winning was very easy for our aunt in the checkers game when we were children. This illustrates how one can win excessively even if the game is fair. Such a scenario could happen if there is a significant difference in skill between players based upon individual efforts made to learn the game or experiences that give one player an advantage. Winning excessively can also be accomplished by having a systematic advantage that creates an in-balance in the game favoring certain players. Such systematic advantage destroys the perception of fairness and indeed is a sign that there is something wrong with the structure of the game.

It is a true statement that winning is contagious, in the sense that learning how to win is often related to your proximity to a winner. Winning builds confidence and enables us to win. Maybe that is what our aunt was thinking when she intentionally lost in checkers. Maybe she knew that winning builds confidence and that what she was giving us was more important than her winning a game in which she had a significant advantage.

The second phase of the Winner's Paradox is brought about by winning excessively, the consequence of which is that no-one wants to play with the excessive winner any more. Just like the card shark, nobody wants to be the sucker and if you are so good, or have such an advantage in the game, you will find yourself without a game.

This is not necessarily a matter of fairness. In fact, we may observe that the winner is winning because of their personal effort and expertise and they are therefore entitled to win. Does it matter why they win? I say this to point out one of the most interesting aspects of the Winner's Paradox. Ultimately it does not matter why someone is winning excessively, the results are exactly the same, no-one wants to play with them. Not because they resent winning or the winner, rather it is because no one likes losing, especially on a continuous basis.

The final phase of the Winner's Paradox is that the winner realizes that the only way they can keep on winning is to have people continue to play. The resulting paradox is that the very thing that makes them a winner, the ability to gain an advantage, is the very thing that will drive others away, therefore eliminating their ability to win. The consequence of such observation leads us to an important revelation about winning. It is in the winner's best interest to see to it that others win as well.

The winner has an understandable bias toward playing, especially in a system like the perpetual Monopoly game in which the winners can almost become as perpetual as the game. For this reason we can assume that the winner always wants to play. Therefore, the primary factor that determines whether or not the game continues revolves around the willingness of the winner to make some concession to help those who are losing excessively. The winner has to balance their desire to win against their desire to have others participate.

We can summarize the Winner's Paradox in the following series of statements:

When the desire to win excessively is greater than their desire to help others win as well, the winner will want to play but there will be no-one to play with and the play will stop.

Desire to win excessively > Desire to help others win as well

does not help and play stops

When the desire to win excessively is equal to the desire to help others win as well the winner is indifferent about playing.

Desire to win excessively = Desire to help others win as well

indifference to helping

When the desire to win excessively is less than the desire to help others win as well, play resumes.

Desire to win excessively < Desire to help others win as well

helps and play resumes

The implications of the Winner's Paradox in a game that requires participation is rather obvious. The winner's moderation determines whether or not play continues, the winner essentially is in control of the game. If the winner wants to fully exploit their advantage they will eventually stop play since those who are losing will eventually not participate due to an increase in their belief that they cannot win. The participation of the loser's will only change if some internal or external factors change for the loser. As already stated some of these internal factors may abate naturally with the passage of time or some event such as an increase in experience. Of course the loser cannot gain experience if they do not play and the winner has a significant impact on this. So there is a relationship between the Winner's Paradox and the Loser's Paradox that ultimately determines what happens in the game.

It becomes obvious that in perpetual Monopoly, participation depends on the moderation of the winner's desire to win continuously or help others and the loser's belief about their ability to win. The winner's willingness to help the loser win stems from an understanding that the key to the game long-term for the winner is participation, to encourage participation the winner helps the loser by giving up some of their advantage in exchange for participation. The loser's belief about whether or not they can win is essentially based on their perception of fairness. To the extent that we get the right balance between the winner's desire for participation and the loser's perception of fairness, the game will continue. This relationship is described in the following statements:

Let Wd = winners desire for participation and Lp = losers perception regarding fairness.

When these are in some approximate equilibrium

Wd ~ Lp

we have a stable game that continues.

It seems that we are overlooking those who do not regard themselves as a winner or a loser. If you remember back to the example of four people playing the Monopoly game in Chapter 1 we talked about the reactions of those playing the game. At the risk of being redundant I will repeat a brief summary of the scenario here.

Assuming that we had four players in the game let's go through each player's emotions and feelings hypothetically after the game has ended. The winner is feeling pretty good as they now have all the money and probably most if not all the property and the satisfaction that they are now king of the Monopoly world. The person who finished second in the game is also feeling pretty good since they beat almost everybody and second place makes them feel that they can win next time, they are probably ready to play again right now. The third place person is consoled by the fact that, while they did not win, at least they did not come in last. They feel somewhat hopeful in their ability to win eventually, they just need more practice. The person who finished last is the real loser which leaves this individual with some serious doubt about their skills and abilities as it relates to the game.

So we have a winner, a loser, and two people somewhere in between, let's call them the middle class of perpetual Monopoly. The middle class in perpetual Monopoly are very important, they are a buffer that helps stabilize the game and encourage participation since the loser can look to this group and believe that they can do better. While the loser may not go from losing to winning, just doing better would be a great encouragement. This middle class is a neutralizing force between the two extremes. A sure sign of coming danger is if this group in the middle starts to disappear, who is the loser going to look up to for encouragement then? If too many in the middle start to identify with the loser they may also quit participating requiring more help from the government. This could cost a lot of money and make the game unstable or even cause it to collapse.

5

THE IMPORTANCE OF PARTICIPATION

Participation in an economic system is critical in order to maintain stability. From a stability point of view it is generally true that the extremes are the focus of most of our attention since it is often the extremes that create instability. The *real* game in our lives is our participation in an economic system, a system that requires participation in order for it to remain stable. Winning the game means different things to different people but is generally defined as "our ability to improve our lives economically by increasing income, the accumulation of wealth, and improved social status". References to "the game" from this point forward are used inter-changeably to refer both to the Monopoly game and our real lives.

We want people to continue to play the game which requires participation, so participation is our proxy for stability. In the perpetual Monopoly game it is the extreme opposite ends of the game experience that create the Winner's and Loser's Paradox, that is why we want to focus primarily on these two groups. If we could create an imaginary game in which we had ninety-nine winners and one loser we can see that so few would lose that the likelihood of the game becoming unstable from lack of participation is very low. Likewise if we had one winner and ninety-nine losers we could see that participation in the game would decline creating instability. If the number of losers in a system is relatively small the impact on stability is relatively small but as the number of losers in the system increases we reach a point in which game participation is affected and the game becomes unstable.

To the extent that the extremes create instability, the number of people between the two extremes create balance. The larger the number of people in the middle, the better it is for stability. In the perpetual Monopoly game it is the middle group that has a buffering effect on the extremes, our perpetual Monopoly game middle class. This group somewhat neutralizes the extremes of the game *if* they are large enough. They generally participate and are interested in playing because they believe they can win, or at least do not consider themselves as losing the game. Their participation is so reliable that we can pretty much ignore them from a stability point of view unless their numbers start changing significantly. If this middle group starts to shrink in numbers, it means they are either moving up in the system becoming more like the winners or moving down in the system and becoming more like the losers.

In an economic system this concept is called social mobility. Social mobility is usually a probability that a person in one social/economic level can move to another social/economic level. It is an important measure of the real opportunity in an economic system. If I say that someone below the poverty line in America has a four percent chance of moving into the lower middle class in the next year that would be a fairly low social mobility rate since four percent is just one out of every twenty-five persons. If on the other hand I were to say that there was a ten percent chance for them to move up or one out of every ten persons in this group, the social/economic mobility would be much better. Moves in the opposite direction are measured by the economic mobility as well. If the players in this middle group have a much higher chance of moving down than they do of moving up it means that the number of people at the bottom is growing and the middle group is shrinking. This would increase instability in the game.

The question for the perpetual Monopoly game is – how do we keep those finishing second or third playing? Will they always play as long as they do not lose too often? It is easy to imagine that in the beginning of the game (a new capitalistic system) it is somewhat easier to win than it is over time since the institutionalized aspects of the game have not taken full effect. Institutionalized refers to something that has become part of the system, a characteristic of the system that is difficult to overcome unless the system is significantly changed.

An important indicator of how the winners, losers, and the middle class are doing in the perpetual Monopoly game is to look at the amount of wealth held by each group. We can observe this by simply calculating the percentage of the total wealth held by each group over time. After several generations (cycles) if we see significant shifts in the proportion of wealth held by a group it means that either the system is favoring this group, the behavior of this group is different than the other groups, or some combination of both of these things. It is very important to realize that it does not matter whether it is a systemic benefit or a behavioral difference that causes the shift, the result is exactly the same. Over time significant shifts can become destabilizing if they are not addressed.

Illustration 5.1

"What's the matter with you people? — Didn't I *tell* you to prosper?"

A common assumption we make in Western economies is that wealthy people have more wealth because they behave differently. This idea is supported by those who have benefited most from the system as well as the government to some extent resulting in average citizens feeling responsible for their lack of achievement. To a large extent we are responsible for our own success but there are other factors at play that are consequences of the design of the system itself.

For those who are more successful we may believe that this group is more ambitious, works harder, works longer, is more intelligent, or is better educated and that is the reason as a group they are more successful. One may alternatively believe that this group is privileged, had better luck, born with a "silver-spoon", had better access, or some other benefit not based on behavior. The truth is probably some combination of these things, the point is, it does not matter. Regardless of WHY they have been able to obtain an advantage, the imbalance of wealth, if significant, will still be a problem.

Regardless of how much wealth one obtains inside an economic structure, it is only valuable because the system continues to function. If the system collapses because of the lack of participation of those groups who have not benefited, the most successful group will come down with the system. Therefore, just as we noticed when we were considering the Winner's Paradox, even the winners lose when the game ends (system collapses). More importantly, the winners lose more than anyone else.

The danger for any social/economic system is that if too many people feel that they are not benefiting, they may quit participating. If enough quit participating the system will fail. If all but the most wealthy withdrew their money from the banks, the banks would fail. If all but the most wealthy did not invest in the stock market, the market would fail. If all but the most wealthy did not pay any taxes, the government would fail.

When you pick up an American dollar you can read the words across the top that say "Federal Reserve Note" which means that the only thing backing up that dollar is the "faith and credit" of the United States government. In other words, our economic system relies on faith. All those who have an issue with "In God We Trust" on currency because it is inconsistent with "separation of church and state" should realize that even if you removed the statement you would still have a system based on faith. So, while you can have separation of church and state you cannot have the separation of faith and state. Even if we were on the old "gold standard" it really wouldn't matter, even the value of gold is based on faith.

So we see that it is participation that makes our economy work. This is the magical unifying truism that brings everyone together, makes everyone interdependent, and should make everyone understand that the real goal in an economic system is to see to it that every group benefits enough to keep them participating. We may act individually within the constraints of the system but in the end we are all dependent on each other.

So let's look at some of our capitalistic systems and see how we are doing. There may be several different ways to measure the sustainability of a social/economic system but the distribution of wealth is an important measuring stick since it is wealth that provides access to most of the benefits of the system. We should look at the percentage of wealth held by each group overtime to see if there are significant shifts in these percentages. Significant shifts in the percentages means that something in the system is either favoring one group or the behavior is different in that group. If it is the system, we should try to fix the system, if it is the behavior we need to work on changing the behaviors of the other groups so they can benefit. Regardless of who in the system is suffering, it is really the problem of everyone in the system. Economic systems should be designed for all participants, not just those with access and influence on the design. Over time the system should be adjusted in order to maintain participation. It is somewhat amusing that our Western genius in capitalistic economic systems is unintentionally holistic if we wish to maintain stability.

There is a tremendous amount of data out there on the web about the wealth and income gaps in America, and in other countries around the world. Many of these sites are connected to organizations or political parties which use these sites to spread their version of the facts. Before we discuss wealth and income gaps we need to define a few things so that we are all on the same page. The first point we should make is that there is a connection between tax policy and the discussion that follows. In America our tax system is similar to other Western democracies but is significantly different than many other countries around the world. Sovereign countries develop their own tax policies, define income and the rates that apply to different types of income. To keep us all from going crazy, the discussion here is related to the US tax system and will be very brief.

First of all we need to understand that there are different types of "income" under our tax system and they are key to understanding the system. We have *earned* income which is from salaries, bonuses, and other payments we receive for doing our jobs. The second component of income is *unearned* income, interest or capital gains. Unearned income is generally from investments, retirement accounts, or savings. Unearned income comes to us in the form of interest, dividends, and gains on stocks and bonds when we sell them.

Secondly we need to take note of the difference between wealth and income. The easiest way to think about wealth is to imagine you sold everything you owned, the total amount of cash you would have is your total wealth. This is different than income in several ways. For example, if you had a job making forty thousand dollars per year and you spent every penny you made on paying your bills, none of the forty thousand dollars would add to your wealth. On the other hand, if after paying all your bills you had ten thousand dollars left over and you put it in a retirement account you would have converted some of your income to wealth. We can also see that wealth can produce *unearned* income from the return on investing money. So we can see that while income and wealth are two different things, income can be converted to wealth and wealth can be converted to income.

The higher your income (*earned or unearned*), the more likely some of it will be converted to wealth. For example, if your income was one million dollars, the chances are much higher that some of it will be converted to wealth by saving or investing. So we see that income can predict wealth since individuals with very high incomes are likely to have more money left over and therefore increase their wealth.

But what if we had no *earned* income, can we still be wealthy? There are many examples of individuals with extreme wealth but no *earned* income. Many of the wealthiest Americans have relatively modest *earned* incomes or no *earned* incomes at all. Watching the news coverage in the fall of 2011 on the passing of Steve Jobs, the founder of Apple, they mentioned he had only taken a salary of one dollar per year for over a decade prior to his passing (I have the utmost admiration for Mr. Jobs so do not think that by using him I am disparaging him or his wealth). How did Mr. Jobs live on one dollar per year of *earned* income? With pay this low he was well below the poverty line which in 2011 which was twenty-two thousand three hundred and fifty dollars for a family of four according to the Department of Health and Human Services[6]. So how did he get by on one dollar a year. Well, Mr. Jobs owned a significant amount of Apple stock and as the stock value increased his wealth increased as well. When Mr. Jobs needed some money, it was very easy to sell some stock and pay his bills. When Mr. Jobs sold this stock he had to pay taxes on the capital gain at probably fifteen percent, considerably lower than most rates of tax on income. So you can see there was not any real incentive to take a larger salary anyway.

In 2011 we had another example of wealth versus income. Warren Buffet, one of the most successful investors in history claimed to have just noticed that his tax rate was lower than that of his secretary. To put this in perspective we should mention that in 2011 the most

---

[6] Federal Register: January 20, 2011 (Volume 76, Number 13). Notices Page 3637-3638 From the Federal Register Online via GPO Access [wais.access.gpo.gov] [DOCID:fr20ja11-76], http://aspe.hhs.gov/poverty/11fedreg.shtml, (October 2011).

likely tax rate for Mr. Buffet was fifteen percent since most of his income would be capital gain income which is *unearned* income. On the other hand if his secretary was single he/she would have paid more than fifteen percent tax if he/she earned more than thirty-four thousand five hundred dollars in a year. I can imagine that Mr. Buffet's secretary probably makes more than this amount. So it is not a surprise that he/she paid taxes at a higher rate than Mr. Buffet would pay on capital gains even if he had millions or billions of dollars in capital gains since the tax on capital gains is the same regardless of the amount. Mr. Buffet is a very smart man and has been around the tax system for a very long time so I seriously doubt that he just now became aware of his tax bracket and the fact that he does not pay a very high percentage.

As an individual who receives very little *earned* income Mr. Buffet would pay mostly capital gain taxes, not the higher *earned* income tax rates. In August of 2011 Mr. Buffet announced that he was in favor of raising the tax rates on the "wealthiest Americans", a concept that the Democrats like and the Republicans seem to hate. As some republicans have correctly pointed out, Mr. Buffet can voluntarily pay as much tax as he wishes since the IRS also takes donations to the US Treasury.

Once we understand these ideas we realize that capital gains taxes on *unearned* income is really a tax on wealth. This is true because to have capital gains on the sale of investments you have to have accumulated the wealth that generated the capital gain. It is important to note that over our long history of collecting taxes in America that capital gains taxes have been lower than *earned* income taxes. In other words, a middle class person would pay a higher tax percentage than the wealthiest of Americans. This is not a recent development. What is the justification for this?

So should we hate the wealthy? First we have to differentiate "the wealthy" as reference to a particular group and wealth as a goal of an economic system. Many people resent "the wealthy" while at the same time benefit from the creation of wealth. Wealth generation is an important characteristic of the capitalistic system and the production of wealth has made our Western system popular all over the world. It has raised our standard of living and benefited most all of us in many ways. So my answer to the question is no, we should not hate, despise, or loath the accumulation of wealth, it is good for all of us. Many who seem to "hate the wealthy" or "despise the rich" are really complaining about the distribution of wealth.

Favoring the accumulation of wealth is woven into our tax system but has a strange bias. It seems that while we all agree, that the creation of wealth is a good thing, the tax system tends to adopt policies that favor the currently wealthy, instead of encouraging the accumulation of wealth among the lower economic classes. Let's take a look at some of these biases starting with some simple tax differences. First let us consider why the taxes on wealth should be lower.

There are a few reasons why the tax on wealth is lower than the tax on earned income. The first argument is that if you over-tax the wealthy, they will just leave your country and move to a place where the taxes are low. Would you live in New York and pay high taxes when you could move to a country that has a zero percent capital gains tax? This is not a joke, there really are places which have a zero percent capital gains tax. Moving from a high tax environment to a low tax environment seems like a logical thing to do and many have done just that in the US and in Europe.

A second point is the argument that if you pay taxes and then invest money you should have a lower tax on the investment earnings because it was already taxed as *earned* income. This is an argument for keeping the capital gains tax rates lower. I find it interesting that this same argument is not applied to interest earned on savings accounts which are taxed as regular income and which are more likely to be held by lower income and middle class individuals and families. Furthermore, in many cases the income that produced the wealth of some of our wealthiest citizens was actually earned by family members several generations ago when there was no income tax.

The third argument is that the wealthy make the economy work better because they are the investors and the job creators. This is not to be ignored and definitely is true in a capitalistic economy. The important thing to remember though is that this would be true no matter who the wealthy were. In other words, if we all took turns playing the role of the wealthy the statement would still be true. So, just because this statement is true does not mean that institutionalized wealth is a good idea. The other thing to remember about this statement is that it is true no matter how the wealth is concentrated. If the same amount of wealth was spread out over a larger group of people, the statement would still be true. So here is an important observation – <u>The fact that we benefit from the creation of wealth does not justify concentrating that wealth in a small fraction of the population</u>. In fact, under ideal circumstances, the wealth would be distributed over a larger part of the population. Under such circumstances, the economic system would still benefit from the role of wealth but would have an important advantage, it would be more stable and social unrest would be contained.

A final argument is that those who are wealthy are special people and they have earned their wealth. While many of the wealthy did not earn their wealth in the traditional sense there are those who have, especially in the case of entrepreneurs. There have been many great entrepreneurs and innovators that have produced an amazing amount of wealth in America and other Western economies. This group is unique, they are winners in the game because they are playing a different game, they create their own game. They have earned it and who are we to take it away from them? They are a special group of people in many ways, so what is so fair about taking their wealth away and giving it to everyone else? We need to answer this question. While it is fashionable to "despise wealth", I notice that few people despise the founder of Apple or the founder of Google who are outrageously wealthy. So what is going on here?

Back to the traditional Monopoly game for a minute. Remember when you played Monopoly when you were a kid and your cousin won. He or she had all the property and money and you lost. Your feelings of defeat were relatively short-lived by the fact that you could wipe the slate clean by starting a new game and try again to win. In the perpetual Monopoly game that we play in real life the game goes on forever and therefore the institutionalized winner and the Loser's Paradox comes into play. For your cousin to win is one thing, but for your cousin's children and their children's children to live with that for generations does not seem fair. After all, what did they do to justify their wealth, power, and access?

In our time we all see what Steve Jobs did and for that, who could despise him or his wealth? I would propose that three generations into the future, if the descendants of Steve Jobs are still living off his wealth and have not really contributed anything beyond consumption, that a lot of people will feel differently. So it is not the accumulation of wealth as much as it is the institutionalization of wealth that brings out the negative reaction.

<u>So what next, do we institute a 100% death tax so that heirs cannot carry the wealth to future generations institutionalizing it forever as an advantage?</u>

At the beginning of this book I said that I was more concerned about framing the question than trying to provide the answers since the answers are complicated and we all need to participate to get it right. There are however a few considerations we should keep in mind while we look for this answer. First of all, we should look at the bigger picture and consider first whether or not we should keep incrementalizing the current system as opposed to making dramatic changes. The best solution in the long term is to not create the problem in the first place, so considering the systemic reason this problem exists and addressing it is most important. Another important thing to remember is that we all wish to create a better future for our children and if we are fortunate enough to accumulate wealth there is nothing evil about the idea of wanting to pass the promise of a better life to our offspring.

Each generation of Americans have witnessed entrepreneurs, inventors, and brilliant minds that have been justly rewarded for the benefit they brought to society. They have added to the quality of life in one way or another. We have many charitable trusts and foundations of the wealthy that have contributed significantly to medicine, environmental problems, technology development, aid to the poor and under-privileged, even to the creation of our national parks. These are not "bad" people. I think the biggest problem for many Americans at the lower end of the system is the difficulty of daily living which include meaningful work, recreation, and the general necessities of life. The downside of generational wealth is that it is based more on family ties than on contributions to society. It is difficult for most Americans to understand the value of mere consumption as a role in life. When the heirs of wealthy produce nothing but consumption, while it undoubtedly good for the overall economy, it also creates a privileged class reminiscent of the feudal era. This phenomena impacts the opportunities for others in the system to become more wealthy.

Some final comments about the accumulation of wealth in an economic system. If wealth generation is the ultimate goal of a social/economic system we can see that the ideal end state would produce a society of wealthy citizens that do not do anything but consume. Who then will produce things for consumption? We have some modern day examples of countries who have approached this state (Saudi Arabia) as well as some historical examples (Rome in middle period of the Roman empire). In such cases the use of foreigners to provide services and the production of things for consumption replaced domestic working classes. Each time humanity has come close to creating the wealthy utopia it has ultimately failed and was overrun by the producers they had come to rely on.

We started out this chapter with the argument that participation in our perpetual Monopoly game relied on participation and that participation was important to maintain balance and keep the system from collapse. So let us now look at some of the data out there that clearly demonstrates a growing wealth gap.

There are numerous resources out there for such data, some are partisan such as the businessinsider.com site and some are part of our government and considered neutral such as the Congressional Budget Office (CBO). I am going to carefully avoid being overly technical in this discussion since I realize that the majority of readers have no interest in statistics and understand that many facts are often misrepresented in statistics. As my father and others have often repeated "figures don't lie, but liars figure". I am very aware of their limitations and am very conscious about misrepresentation so I have been careful and completely fair about the presentation here. As far as the wealth gap is concerned, no matter which source you use to investigate it, you will find agreement that it exists, you will also find some clever arguments at interpreting the facts to coincide with different political views and you will find even more disagreement about what it means.

If you are wondering where I am politically, I will confess that I am independent but I am not sure what that means today. So I must say it this way, I think and vote independently of any party affiliation, including identifying with what is today called "Independents".

6

SO LET'S LOOK AT SOME INTERESTING NUMBERS

I will apologize in advance for this chapter. If you are like most people you do not really like reading through a bunch of numbers, and this chapter has plenty. The reason it is important to put them here is that the evidence of what is happening in America is supported by analysis of the numbers, without which we are providing only an opinion, and opinions are cheap. In addition, while there are significant differences in wealth and income along gender and racial divides they are not covered here since my interest is in providing an overall view of the problem. The fact that they these differences are not discussed in any detail does not mean that they are any less important.

If you would like to skip this chapter and come back to it, you are welcome to do so. The flow of the book will really not change as long as you read the last two paragraphs in this chapter. You can come back to the chapter as desired to dig into the details. Or do what we usually do... just look at the pictures.

According to the Institute for Policy Studies, the wealth distribution in America in 2007 looked a little lopsided. The top one percent of Americans held almost thirty-four percent (33.8%) of the wealth, the next nine percent of Americans held almost thirty-eight percent (37.7%), the next forty percent of Americans held twenty-six percent, and the bottom fifty percent of Americans held two and a half percent. It is important to note that the Institute for Policy Studies (IPS) is generally viewed as a left leaning (Democratic) organization. This does not necessarily mean their numbers are wrong, this just may be the reason they are interested in the wealth gap topic.

Another chart from IPS on the Business Insider website[7] shows the ownership of U.S. stock, bond, and mutual funds in 2007. As we discussed in the prior section, ownership of investments is directly connected to the accumulation of wealth. Therefore, we would expect some agreement between this breakdown and the one just given above. According to this chart the top one percent of Americans has over fifty-nine percent (59.1%) of the total investments, the next nine percent has over thirty-nine percent (39.4%) of investments, the next forty percent have over nine percent (9.3%), and the bottom fifty percent of Americans own only one-half percent (0.5%) of the

---

[7] Gus Lubin. "15 Mind-Blowing Facts About Wealth And Inequality In America". April 9, 2010, available at http://www.businessinsider.com/15-charts-about-wealth-and-inequality-in-america-2010-4, (October 2011).

investments in U.S. stock, bonds, and mutual funds. To make these easier to compare Table 6.1 below puts them side by side.

Table 6.1 - Comparison of Total Wealth and Total Investment in U.S. stock, bonds, and mutual funds in 2007

Group	Percentiles	Percent of Total Wealth	Percent of Investment
Top 1%	99% to 100%	33.8%	59.1%
Next 9%	90% to 99%	37.7%	39.4%
Next 40%	50% to 90%	26.0%	9.3%
Bottom 50%	0% to 50%	2.5%	0.5%

There are several interesting observations we can make about these numbers. Notice that the top one percent owns a larger percentage of total investments than they do of total wealth and the bottom ninety percent are just the opposite. One of the reasons for this is that a significant part of the wealth in the lower ninety percent of Americans is made up of equity in their homes. These numbers have changed somewhat since 2008 because of the decline in home values that has destroyed a significant amount of the wealth held by the bottom ninety percent of Americans.

If you do some adding of these percentages you realize that the bottom ninety percent of Americans held only twenty-eight and one-half percent of wealth and about ten percent (9.8%) of investment. After 2008, the wealth and investment of this lower ninety percent group has declined because of the collapse in home values. Data from 2007[8] show that sixty-one and one-half percent of the wealth held by the bottom ninety percent of the U.S. households was in their homes.

After the collapse in home values, the ability of those over fifty years old to retire will be delayed as many of them will have to work well into their senior years in order to make up for the loss of equity in their homes which many cash in on at retirement by downsizing....... this generation is not retiring anytime soon! The "greatest" generation of seniors is going to be replaced by the "poorest" generation of American retirees in our recent history.

To be fair with sources here let's now look at what should be a neutral source, the Federal Reserve Board and data collected under a Republican administration in The Survey of Consumer Finances[9] presented in Table 6.2.

If you add some numbers up here you will find that these results are pretty much in agreement with the ones presented by IPS even though the one source is 2004 and the other is 2007. Besides the obvious difference of the year that the data was collected there

---

[8] E. N. Wolff, (2010). "Recent trends in household wealth in the United States: Rising debt and the middle-class squeeze - an update to 2007". Working Paper No. 589. Annandale-on-Hudson, NY: The Levy Economics Institute of Bard College. Also available at http://sociology.ucsc.edu/whorulesamerica/power/wealth.html (October 2011).

[9] Brian K. Bucks, Arthur B. Kennickell, and Kevin B. Moore. "Recent Changes in U.S. Family Finances: Evidence from the 2001 and 2004 Survey of Consumer Finances". Available at http://www.federalreserve.gov/pubs/oss/oss2/2004/bull0206.pdf, (October 2011).

is also a slight difference in the breakdown of the categories. The top one percent is over thirty-four percent is (34.3%) in the Federal Reserve data vs. slightly less in the IPS data (33.8%), the next nine percent is thirty-seven percent for the Federal Reserve vs. almost thirty-eight percent (37.7%) for IPS, the next fifty percent in the Fed Reserve data is twenty-eight and one-half percent while the next forty percent in the IPS data is twenty-six percent, and the bottom forty percent in the Federal Reserve data is barely above zero (0.2%), while the bottom fifty percent in the IPS data is two and one-half percent.

<u>Table 6.2 - Percentage of total wealth held by US households in 2004</u>

	Percentile	Percent of total wealth
Top 1%	99% - 100%	34.3%
Next 4%	95% - 99%	24.6%
Next 5%	90% - 95%	12.3%
Next 10%	80% - 90%	13.4%
Next 20%	60% 80%	11.3%
Next 20%	40% - 60%	3.8%
Bottom 40%	0% - 40%	0.2%

Overall these numbers are close enough to make a strong argument for a significant wealth gap in America. There are numerous other sources on the web that show similar numbers and not one single site seriously contradicts the Federal Reserve data.

Interestingly enough there are several individuals contributing good research in the area of wealth distribution. Michel Norton of Harvard Business School and Dan Arieli of Duke University teamed up to publish an interesting article titled "Building a Better America - One Wealth Quintile at a Time"[10]. In this article, the authors maintain that both sides of the political divide in America want a better distribution of wealth. Their findings were that "All demographic groups—even those not usually associated with wealth redistribution such as Republicans and the wealthy—desired a more equal distribution of wealth than the status quo".

So there we go............... problem solved…....right?

In this most interesting and insightful article they presented three different models of wealth distribution and asked individuals to select which one they preferred. All three models presented the distributions of wealth in quintiles, 1/5 of the population in each group. The three models consisted of one based on America's actual *wealth* distribution data, one based on Swedish *income* distribution data, and one that is the equality baseline in which all groups were exactly equal.

Subjects were presented these three models without identifying labels and asked which one they prefer. Forty-seven percent favored the Swedish income distribution, forty-three percent favored the equal distribution, and ten percent favored the American distribution. As presented in Table 6.3, the outcome of this was not surprising since even though most people prefer to be wealthy most think that the high concentration is unfair. There were, however,

---

[10] Michael Norton and Dan Arieli. "Building a Better America – One Wealth Quintile at a Time". Perspectives on Psychological Science. February 2011, 6(1) 9-12. Available at http://duke.edu/~dandan/Papers/BuildingBetterAmerica.pdf, (October 2011).

some surprising outcomes in the research regarding preferences of the participants along demographic lines. Regardless of gender, political affiliation, or income level, the Sweden income distribution was favored. No group favored the U.S. distribution or the equal distribution. This indicates that Americans understand the rational of differences in wealth accumulation based on differences in talent, hard work, and even inheritance.

Table 6.3 - Three models of income distribution

Percentile	American distribution	Sweden distribution	Equal distribution
80%-100%	84.0%	36.0%	20.0%
60%-80%	11.0%	21.0%	20.0%
40%-60%	4.0%	18.0%	20.0%
20%-40%	0.2%	15.0%	20.0%
0%-20%	0.1%	11.0%	20.0%

As is often the case with sound bites and published information, if you do not read it carefully you may miss something that is important. The one fault in this article is that Sweden *income* distribution data was used instead of wealth distribution data. Therefore, you may incorrectly conclude that wealth in Sweden is better distributed than in the U.S. when in fact that is not the case[11]. I might add that the author's use of the income data does not affect the legitimacy of the article or the

---

[11] G. William Domhoff. "Wealth, Income, and Power", September 2005 (updated October 2011), Available at http://sociology.ucsc.edu/whorulesamerica/power/wealth.html, (October 2011). In Sweden over fifty-eight percent (58.6%) of the wealth is held by the top ten percent of the population.

message from a preference point of view since the authors could have used a purely fictitious distribution instead of the Sweden income distribution and had the same outcome.

Now we can ask the question – how do you control wealth distribution? The answer to this is not so simple. As I said earlier the easiest way to solve a problem is to prevent it from ever occurring in the first place. With regard to the wealth gap we have several options. One of the options is to tax the wealthy at a very high rate on *earned* income, investment income, and on inheritance. There is no doubt that this will reduce the wealth, but it will just mean that the government now has all the wealth and what will they do with it?..... they do not have a very good record managing tax money. I would like to think that it would be applied to our deficit but based on history it is more likely to be spent on programs....some good, some bad, and some very very bad..

Another option is the Robin Hood approach which is already built into our tax system through transfer payments such as Earned Income Credit. Under the Robin Hood approach we take from the rich and give to the poor. While some people like this idea, it is not as satisfying as having a system that would enable more players in the game to accumulate more wealth and not have it given to them through transfer payments by the mother of all inefficiency, our federal government.

Some of the consequences of aggressive taxes on the rich have already been mentioned. Given our global environment we must realize that there are countries out there in the business of attracting the wealthy with attractive policies toward wealth. There is sort of a "free agent" aspect to being wealthy today, you are recruited by friendly tax and investment policies just like sport stars or large corporations. If you were taxed at seventy or eighty percent of your income or heavily taxed on your wealth, would you consider moving to another country?

We have to regress for a minute in the interest of fairness. As we mentioned earlier there is a relationship between higher income and the accumulation of wealth. Remember the example of different income levels and the observation that as income increases an individual is more likely to accumulate wealth since it does not take all their income to pay their bills. We should recognize that in America the higher *income* earners pay the majority of the taxes.[12] Table 6.4 provides some useful insight into this fact. Income in this table includes *earned* and *unearned* income.

Table 6.4 - Percentage of INCOME taxes paid by different income groups

Bracket	Percent paid	Average Income
Top 1%	40.4%	$410,096
Top 5%	60.6%	$160,041
Top 10%	70.2%	$113,018
Top 25%	86.6%	$66,532
Top 50%	97.1%	$32,879
Bottom 50%	2.9%	<$32,879

---

[12] Tom Murse "How Much Do You Pay in Income Taxes? - Individual Income Tax Rates and Shares Explained". August 24, 2011. Available at http://usgovinfo.about.com/od/incometaxandtheirs/a/who-pays-most-income-tax.htm

As you can see from looking at these numbers the higher incomes pay a majority of the income taxes. In fact the top one percent pay over forty percent (40.4%) of income taxes, the top ten percent as a group pay over seventy percent (70.2 %), the top fifty percent as a group pay over ninety-seven percent (97.1%) leaving the bottom fifty percent of income earners paying only about three percent (2.9%) of the bill.

So that we are not confused, we must realize that the US government collects all types of taxes including income, payroll taxes, corporate taxes, excise taxes, and many other including a federal tax on our phone bill. In fact the income taxes, according to the 2008 Congressional Budget Office data, are only forty three percent of the total taxes collected.

<u>Wealth gap over time</u>

Now that we have established that there is a wealth gap in the U.S. we should look at the trend over time and see if the gap is changing. For this information we will look to the work of E.N. Wolff and The Levy Economics Institute of Bard College. In two different articles Professor Wolff looked at the wealth distribution covering the period of 1922 to 2007.[13,14]

Figure 6.1 is based on this research and shows that the high point in the amount of wealth held by the top one percent during this period was over forty-four

---

[13] E. N. Wolff, (2010). "Recent trends in household wealth in the United States: Rising debt and the middle-class squeeze - an update to 2007". Working Paper No. 589. Annandale-on-Hudson, NY: The Levy Economics Institute of Bard College. Also available at http://sociology.ucsc.edu/whorulesamerica/power/wealth.html (October 2011).

[14] E. N. Wolff. (1996). Top Heavy. New York: The New Press.

percent (44.2%) in 1929 just before the stock market crash. The low point of total wealth held by this group was in 1976 when it dipped to about twenty percent (19.9%). Since 1976 the general trend is higher until just before the 2000 crash when it topped out over thirty eight percent. After the 2000 crash the gap rose again from just over thirty-three percent (33.4%) to almost thirty-five percent (34.6%) in 2007. Since the majority of the wealth held by this group is in investments, it is no surprise that the trend follows the stock market.

Figure 6.1

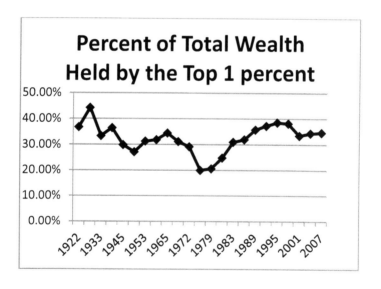

While this is the latest data available, things have probably changed since 2007. Ironically, the percentage of wealth held by the top one percent has probably increased since 2007 based on the difference between the stock market recovery and the recovery in housing. Even though the market dropped significantly in 2008 and 2009, by the fall of 2010 the market had recovered significantly with the DOW index back close to 12,000. This means that the top one percent, who held most of their wealth in the market, probably did much better than the bottom ninety percent which held most of their wealth in their homes.

Wealth gap in older European democracies

We know there is a significant wealth gap in America and we know that it has existed over a long period of time, but how do we compare to the older democracies of Europe? In a 2006 study by the World Institute for Development Economics Research[15] titled "The World Distribution of Household Wealth", data from 2000 was used to compare the United Sates to other Western countries. This study looked at the percent of wealth held by the top ten percent of the population in each country. The results of this comparison show that America has a higher concentration of wealth than any of our European counterparts with the exception of Switzerland. Switzerland was the highest at over seventy-on percent (71.3%) followed by America at almost seventy percent (69.8%), Denmark at sixty-five percent, France at sixty-one percent, Sweden at almost fifty-nine percent (58.6%), United Kingdom at fifty-six percent, Canada at fifty-three, Norway at over fifty percent (50.5%), Germany at over forty-four percent (44.4%), and Finland at just over forty-two percent (42.3%).

---

[15] J.B. Davies, S. Sandstrom, A. Shorrocks, E.N. Wolff (2006). "The World Distribution of Household Wealth". Helsinki: World Institute for Development Economics Research.

It is interesting to note that when we look at <u>income distribution</u> we see a similar pattern with America near the top of countries with the largest income disparities. Economists use the Gini index[16], a mathematical ratio that puts all countries on the same scale, to measure income inequality. The higher the Gini index, the higher the income inequality. According to the Central intelligence Agency World Fact Book[17] (2010), the United States was ninety fifth on a list of one hundred and thirty-four countries reported. This indicates that the U.S. had the most unequal income distribution of the Western Democracies. Table 6.5

<u>Table 6.5 - Income and Wealth Distribution Comparison</u>

	Gini Index for income inequality	Year Gini was calculated	Percent of Wealth held by top 10%
United States	45.0	2007	69.8%
UK	34.0	2005	56.0%
Switzerland	33.7	2008	71.3%
France	32.7	2008	61.0%
Canada	32.1	2005	53.0%
Denmark	29.0	2007	65.0%
Germany	27.0	2006	44.4%
Finland	26.8	2008	42.3%
Norway	25.0	2008	50.5%
Sweden	23.0	2005	58.6%

---

[16] Wikipedia. Gini Coefficient. Available at http://en.wikipedia.org/wiki/ Gini_coefficient.
[17] Central Intelligence Agency (2010). World Factbook: Country Comparison: Distribution of family income - Gini index. Available at https://www.cia.gov/ library/publications/the-world-factbook/rankorder/2172rank.html, (October 2011).

shows the Gini index for household income, the year the Gini index was calculated, and the percentage of wealth held by the ten percent of each population in 2000. When we compare ourselves to the same list of countries as we did for wealth distribution we have the following results.

<u>Social mobility in the US</u>

Part of the American dream and part of the reason why high levels of wealth and income have not been a big problem in the U.S. may be that many Americans believe that they can achieve higher income and wealth too. Social mobility refers to the ability of economic classes within a population to move from one level to another. So a comparison of the social mobility of Americans would show, over time, what the chances are that a person will move from one economic class or group to another. There is no doubt that some can and do, but research shows that social mobility has been declining for decades.

Using Social Security System micro data since 1937, Wojciech Kopczuk of Columbia, Emmanuel Saez from UC Berkeley, and Jae Song of the Social Security Administration collaborated on a paper in 2007[18] to study several aspects of social mobility. The findings reported in the paper indicate that the probability of moving up or down has leveled off significantly since

---

[18] Wojciech Kopczuk, Emmanuel Saez, Jae Song. "Uncovering the American Dream: Inequality and Mobility in Social Security Earnings Data since 1937", NBER Working Paper No. 13345 Issued in August 2007. Available at http://www.nber.org/papers/w13345, Figure 4B (October 2011).

1960. Since that time the probability of moving up or down has been holding at around four percent which is not a very encouraging number for most Americans. Figure 6.2 below is a reprint from Figure 4B of the paper. The four percent mobility number means that in any given year the probability of moving from the bottom forty percent to the top sixty percent group is only four percent. Once there you have a four percent chance of returning to the lower group in one year. What the chart clearly demonstrates is that movement between the lower and upper income groups (based on the lower forty percent and upper sixty percent) is stagnant therefore your chances, based on the numbers are not that good.

Perhaps the most disturbing observation in the data is what has happened to the trend line for upward mobility (the solid black line) and the line for downward mobility (the hyphenated line) over time. As you can see, the upward mobility line was above the downward mobility line up until about 1970. This means that up until about 1970 Americans had a better chance of moving up in economic class than down. They had a better chance of moving from the bottom forty percent to the upper sixty percent than they did of moving from the upper sixty percent to the bottom forty percent. During the eighties the upward mobility line remained slightly higher but beginning in the nineties it clearly flattened out and even went upside down. <u>When these lines are inverted it means that Americans are more like to move from the middle class to lower classes</u>, therefore shrinking the middle class and creating instability. The implications of this is tremendous, this signifies the death of the American dream and the fact that our system is broken.

Figure 6.2

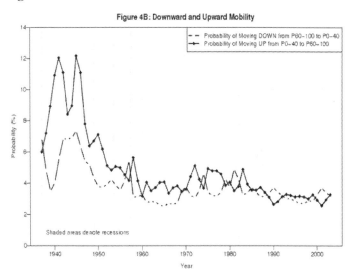

Some other interesting information from this study is that the proportion of total income going to the bottom eighty percent of wage earners has been declining since around 1950. The eighty to ninety-five percent category has been holding steady, and the only group that has increased since 1950 is the top five percent with the top one percent getting most of that.

The bottom line is we all want to have a better life, and in general we do not want to blame the wealthy for enjoying the good life, or wanting to stay there. Most of us would want the same thing, how many William Borden's have you seen? Many Americans aspire to improve their economic position in life and pass it on to their kids who hopefully, can even have a better life. Most of us understand that wealth and income is not evil, nor is the reasonable and legal pursuit of wealth and income. It is all about fair play, and if we all have a reasonable chance of improving our lot in life we understand how different people can achieve different goals, especially since people have many different goals when it comes to wealth and income. Some of our wealthy have been utterly gracious with their wealth and some have maintained a relatively modest life style in spite of their wealth (see Steve Jobs biography for example). We can no more put all the wealthy in one category than we can the members of any other income or wealth group.

From the information presented in this chapter we can conclude that wealth and income are highly concentrated in America, more so than in any other developed country in the world. Our ideals of capitalism and democracy which seemed to promise economic benefits to a larger number of citizens do not seem to be working after several generations. Just like in the perpetual Monopoly game it seems that some are winning excessively and some are losing excessively and more and more Americans are checking out of the Adam Smith hotel. We are becoming a Plutonomy as described by Citigroup analyst Ajay Kapur in 2005[19]. A Plutonomy refers to a society where the majority of the wealth is controlled by an ever-shrinking minority; as such, the economic growth of that society becomes dependent on the fortunes of that same wealthy minority. In his memos Ajay Kapur estimates that in 2005, the richest twenty percent may have been responsible for sixty percent of total spending. This is

---

[19] Robert Frank. "Plutonomics", The Wall Street Journal digital network, WSJ Blogs, January 8, 2007. Available at http://blogs.wsj.com/wealth/2007/01/08/plutonomics/, (October 2011).

some really interesting reading if you can find it on the web, certain sites have pulled it down due to the high level of controversy over the subject matter and the obvious problems associated with wider distribution... This is something you will never see in major media sources............... Makes you wonder doesn't it? The Plutonomy of America also explains the upswing in consumer spending in-spite of the fact that many Americans are losing their homes in the highest foreclosure rates in our history.

7

BEYOND *PERPETUAL* MONOPOLY TO THE CASINO

Imagine for a moment that we allow perpetual Monopoly players to join forces and form a company. This would allow players to pool their winner's advantage in pursuit of accumulating more wealth. Of course we would have to make another new rule for this but think of the benefits. As the real estate on the game board goes vertical we could use their help managing a bigger and bigger game, it only makes sense to team up like this.

Over time these small companies become larger and larger until the perpetual Monopoly conglomerate is born. When this happens, even wealthy individual players will be threatened by the larger economic entities, and to protect themselves and their wealth they will have to join one or start their own corporation. If they choose to pool some of their money with an existing corporation, they will simply become part of the corporation, I guess you might say they would buy a "share" .... OMG it looks like we have a stock market. So now that we have corporations, a stock market, and a bank in the perpetual Monopoly game it is really starting to look like the America we recognize.

Many of us today think that the stock market was born before our country was founded, it certainly seems that way when you observe how Washington, most of our politicians, and the media react to every little twist and turn in the market as if it is the proverbial heartbeat of America. The market was actually formed a few decades after America, and it was well over a century later before it looked anything like the market of today. The reason it took so long to take off is simple, a stock market really needs participation to work correctly.

In the 1800's there was <u>not</u> a lot of money lying around since our entire financial system was very under-developed, there were relatively few banks, and they were only used by relatively few people. Compared to what it is today we would hardly recognize it. Just like computers no one really thought they needed one until one was available. People slowly began to realize the benefits of having a bank, and for that matter a financial system. One of the main reasons we needed a bank in America was to run the government. It is one thing to have the citizens running around trading coins, corn and chickens, it is a whole different matter when you think about a government doing this to pay bills.

The first stock market was in Belgium in 1531 with Amsterdam, Paris, and Berlin following in 1602. London did not have a market until around 1725 and the young United States in 1792. The first exchange in America was outdoors under a buttonwood tree in Castle Garden which is now Battery Park and was formed shortly after the banner day in 1791 when one hundred shares changed hands privately. Rather minuscule when you consider that the average daily volume on the New York Stock Exchange in 2011 is almost 1.9 billion shares. The original exchange had twenty-four participants who signed an agreement detailing the rules, fees, and regulations of trading. By 1800 there were only twenty publicly traded corporations in America, the first being the Bank of New York….. the ominous beginning of government graft.

The original Stock Exchange Office on Wall Street held noon-time auctions of securities to the highest bidder. They were known as the Curbstone Brokers. It was not until 1919 that the Curbstone Brokers built a building and moved the exchange inside. In 1928 they renamed themselves the New York Curb Exchange just one year before the 1929 market crash. It was not until 1953 that the name was changed to the American Stock Exchange[20] then later the New York Stock Exchange.

So you see, while many of us today were thinking that the founding fathers asked permission of the *marketeers* before writing the constitution, things actually happened in reverse. The stock market developed after the United States and, by the way, after our democracy was born. An even greater surprise is the fact that the stock market was not really a significant influence until

---

[20] A to Z Investments "Wall Street & Stock Market History" Available at http://www.atozinvestments.com/history-of-wall-street.html, (October 2011).

around 1920 and for most American's, was not part of their economic life until the popularity of mutual funds in the 1980's.

The first significant market crash was not a crash at all according to the words used to describe it; it is referred to as the Panic of 1836. The market was very small, very private, had few participants, and did not really influence the lives of many Americans. For these reasons it was hardly noticed, and for most of America it was not noticed at all. As we all know the next significant crash was going to be considerably different.

It is interesting that once the market moved inside the speculative run-up to the 1929 crash began. Maybe we can speculate as to the causes of this. Was it the sign on the front of the building, the furniture and decorating, the permanent location, or the fact that people preferred not to stand out in the weather, in the cold, mud, rain, or heat to trade stocks. Whatever it was the trading volume zoomed. Maybe it was paying for the building that caused the market participants to encourage more trading; somebody had to make enough trading commissions to pay for the new digs.

As trading activity increased, some people began making money, a lot of money. Eventually more and more people began to realize that it was not making or producing something that mattered, all they needed to do was buy some stock and they could become rich too. You have to admit, this is a little more appealing than putting in the hard work that it takes to produce something that people use or consume. You can also imagine that everyone who had a few extra bucks thought this idea was pretty appealing, so many traded in their work boots for a little speculation. Because more and more people participated, the prices of stocks were driven up until they really had no relationship to the value of the corporations at all. Like a gigantic Ponzi scheme, the market had become an entity unto itself and reality became distorted by the feeding frenzy.

The fact was the investor did not care about this, hell, they may not even know the company, and for that matter the company may not have even been real, THEY JUST WANTED THE STOCK TO GO UP SO THEY COULD BECOME RICH. It is sounding more and more like the market we know today. As we all know the market eventually crashed, the speculation on value that did not exist all came tumbling down. While many had lost money that they had made in the market, many lost money that they had really earned the hard way, and it was a long time before America recovered.

So how does the stock market work anyway?

Let's go back to a time before there was a market and imagine why we needed one anyway. It all started out with the simple idea that we needed a way to easily transfer ownership of a company. As companies or corporations became larger it was much more convenient to transfer ownership with a stock certificate, which represented a share for the company, rather than going through a much more complicated legal process to do so. This made it very easy to transfer ownership by trading these certificates for cash or some other stock, all we had to do was sign over the stock certificate to someone else and we were done, no lawyers, no delay.

Once we were comfortable with holding stock certificates to represent company ownership interest an even more interesting idea developed. What if we simply formed a new company by selling stock certificates in the first place? This idea was the beginning of public financing of corporations. In the beginning of this process, only financiers who understood the process participated and it was a way for them to hold interest and transfer their interest among themselves without much hoopla. So far so good…. still with me?

If a group of people were to form a small business today they would all put their money together and start the company. A likely alternative is that they would put some of their own money together, borrow some more money from a bank and start the business. What if they did not want to go to the bank or what if there were not any banks, at least any banks that would lend them money? How would they get the money then? One of the options, if the company is big enough and if you have enough big players, is to go for public financing of your company.

I teach business students at the senior level and I always quiz them verbally on what they know about the stock market and how it works. Maybe one or two students in a class of forty have a clue to how it works. Even adults who have been buying stock through their retirement accounts for decades do not understand some of the most important concepts. So I am going to try to make sense out of it in the next few paragraphs.

I ask this question to students all the time, see if you know the answer.

Let's imagine that General Electric wanted to raise one hundred million dollars and did so through a public sale of stock. Imagine also that you think GE is a good company so you bought ten thousand dollars of this stock. When does GE pay you back?

So what……. you think I am going to put the answer here?

Back to our discussion of the stock market. So you can see that the stock market was born because there was a need for a place which private citizen financiers could trade stock among themselves. It was a logical progression of the idea behind the creation of money, which was to make it easier for people to trade among themselves. Instead of going to market to trade your chickens for some vegetables, you can sell your chickens today for money and buy the vegetables tomorrow with the money.

Ok, I feel the distraction……. here is the answer. General Electric <u>never</u> pays back your ten thousand dollar investment, even if the company fails and they lose all your money. If you want your money back, you take your GE stock and sell it for whatever you can get, in other words you have to find someone to buy your stock. Hence we have stock trading…. but back to GE for a minute. You probably picked up on an amazing thing about now, selling stock is a lot better than borrowing money from a bank. I mean, if you borrow money from a bank you have to pay it back, if you sell stock you never have to pay it back, even if you lose all the money. You are probably thinking that you want to build that new dream house now and instead of going to the bank, you want to sell stock in your new house. Who cares if the people who buy the stock own your house, would you rather they own it or the bank?

Considering that stockholders cannot <u>foreclose</u> on stock and the bank can foreclose on your loan, the choice is simple. If the economy tanks and the price of your home stock falls, you would indeed have some interesting options. As the CEO of your home you could do the same thing GE can do when the market declines, buy shares of your house back at a big discount and sell them back into the market when things get better. Your mortgage problems are so simple…. you just need the right tool.

Throughout this section I use General Electric (GE) in my examples to explain the workings of the stock market. I am not picking on GE, actually I think they are a good company, I am merely using them in the examples because they are a household name. As it turns out I have some had news on the house deal I discussed in the last paragraph. Not just anyone can raise money by selling stock. Only some people/companies are allowed to do this because it would cause a lot of problems if too many people lost money on their stock, they wouldn't buy anymore, and the market for stock would collapse. Oddly enough, there are no qualifications for buying stock, anyone can buy it even if they know absolutely nothing about the market or how it works. For most individuals the stock market is like a casino, and just like the casino they often lose and some lose big. In fact it is worse than a casino because when you go to the casino you know you are gambling and realize you will probably lose your money. With the cooperation of the US Government, the marketeers have convinced most Americans that they are investing when in fact most of them are gambling.

So who gets to sell stock? Only the largest companies can sell stock to the public. Small companies cannot do this because they are regarded as too unstable, too many of them fail. Large companies fail too, but much less often than small ones. Since I explained the big benefit to GE selling stock and never having to pay it back, let's look at the down side. When GE sells the hundred million dollars of stock they initially get all the money, but as the stock is traded over decades and goes up GE does not get any of the gain. Since the GE stock is traded among individuals after the initial sale to the public in transactions that are outside of GE, GE does not benefit directly when their stock goes from say five dollars to twenty-five dollars per share. All the profit from this goes to the individuals who traded the stock. Likewise when GE stock drops from twenty-five dollars to fifteen dollars per share GE does not lose money, the individuals who traded the stock do. Hate to bore you with these details but in order for things to get better we need to make sure we understand the problem.

There are some serious problems with the stock market. As we noticed in the 1929 crash, if prices for stock are driven up by speculation beyond the real values, the market can become very unstable and perhaps even crash. And YES the stock market did CRASH in 2008 even though the industry has carefully avoided using the term. Anytime the market loses half its value it is a crash, not a down turn. Millions of Americans who had money in the market lost half the value of their retirement accounts in the crash. There was a tremendous wealth transfer from unsophisticated small investors to the very sophisticated investors who better understand the market and how to trade. These small investors are Americans who had money in the market through their retirement programs such as 401k's, 403b's, IRA's and many other individual and company sponsored plans.

If you go to work for a company with a retirement plan you contribute your own money and usually the company matches all or part of your contribution. You then invest the money through the company that sold the plan to the company. Large insurance companies are the largest providers of private retirement plans in America. The problem with the plans is that the investment options are usually very limited and highly biased to a market that goes up not down. Consequently when the market goes down there is no way to make money in these plans and if you just set there you will see your account value crash right along with the market. About all you can do to avoid this in these retirement plans is to move all your money from the mutual funds to things like treasury bills or money market options which are usually available.

For more sophisticated investors there are many options for them to profit when the market goes down. I will not cover them in any detail here but when you sell a stock short you actually make money when it goes down. There are also many other options for these more sophisticated investors such as buying put options, derivatives, short ETFs (exchange traded funds), bear mutual funds, and even volatility indexes. I know that this is GREEK to most everyone and that is the point of bringing this up. THE STOCK MARKET IS NOT DESIGNED TO BE FAIR TO THE SMALLER INVESTOR and for many small investors it is a disaster. For the more sophisticated investment community, taking money from the small investor is like taking candy from children. It is not a level playing field and was NEVER intended to be, you must understand this. Shame on the US Government for encouraging Americans to invest in the stock market under the pretense of regulation by the Securities and Exchange Commission who cannot even regulate themselves much less the market.

The collaboration between our government and the financial industry has assured participation of many American small investors through retirement accounts. This increase in participation has created more opportunities to make money on Wall Street, unfortunately these opportunities are for the more sophisticated investors. Participation in the market sky-rocked in the 1980's as these type of retirement plans flourished along with the introduction of mutual funds as the solution for the small investor. The designers simply over-looked the fact that the restricted mutual fund choices of most retirement plans coupled with the unsophisticated investor's lack of understanding of the market would mean that in a major market decline Americans were going to take a beating. Even after the 2000 decline in the market no adjustments were made.

In the 2008 crash it was totally devastating to many Americans who had their life's retirement savings on the table in the government sponsored casino. Every month billions of American retirement dollars flow into the market through the purchasing of mutual funds through retirement plans. It is just like a Brink's truck delivery to the bank of Wall Street. Over time some of these dollars will earn money but the risk is high, and the majority of the money made on Wall Street will always go to the more sophisticated investors.

In the fall of 2011 the Occupy Wall Street protests began. When the media first approached some of the protestor's and asked them what they were protesting they really could not give a clear answer, eventually they did say "corporate greed". I would say that it was the financial industry that destroyed the housing market and I guess you can say that is corporate alright, but they are missing some of the other elements that contributed significantly such as the role of institutionalized wealth that drives the financial industry, the corporate board rooms, and the political machinery that keeps them in the money. There is a tremendous impact on our world from the wealth cycle of WEALTH➔ ACCESS➔ INFLUENCE➔MORE WEALTH that drives the financial markets, corporations, and politics. We will talk more about this later.

Another problem with the market is that it no longer is simply a way for people to easily buy or sell ownership in companies they are interested in owning. The market has become its own industry, its own business, and is largely detached from the companies that are traded on the exchange. The companies are merely an enabling force, an opportunity to trade for profit. They are the dogs at the race track or the sports game in Los Vegas, nothing more. Those who run the market really do not care if companies survive except to the extent that having companies to trade is necessary in order to have a market. If there were no companies to trade, the market would simply trade something else. The start of the 2008 crash was the short selling of bank stocks that created a feeding frenzy driving the market down all the while making money for the short selling, in the fact the lower it went the more the short sellers made.

The financial industry is intangible in many ways and this is the problem with individuals and governments understanding them. The industry produces no tangible product or service but manages to extract much of the profits out of our economy and away from those who do, simply by trading electronic paper. A growing part of our economy has become the market! The market was supposed to make the economy work better by providing easier means of buying and selling of corporate interests, make it easier to raise capital, encouraging efficiency, and provide a way for individuals to participate in the American dream. Through the market, the average American could invest in the large corporation and participate in the profits of the corporation, after all if the corporate profits go up, the stock should go up too….. right? Today the market can go down while corporate profits go up – this is just how disconnected it is from reality and another indication of how far we have moved from what was a good idea.

I think the Occupy Wall Street protestors feel this disconnect and their conclusion is that somehow the Wall Street crowd, the financial industry and the corporate world has conspired against them. They are right - I mean the peasants are right - except that they should also be camped out in front of the White House and Congress. The government has played a significant role. Just remember this; no one that played a role in the disaster has been put in jail because they did not, at least in the eyes of the government, break any laws. How can this be? This can "be" because there is a relationship between government, corporations, Wall Street, and the rest of the financial industry.

Given the structure of the market and having an understanding of the gunslinger atmosphere, it is not so difficult to understand why the greatest Ponzi scheme was pulled off right under the noses of the largest and most sophisticated financial environment on the planet. As we have all heard, Bernie Madoff stole over sixty billion dollars of other people's money. As former head of the Nasdaq exchange he was the perfect "confidence man", he had the background, he knew the weaknesses in the system and he easily exploited them for his benefit. I think it was just a small step for Bernie to go from legitimate trading to the Ponzi scheme because in reality the market is pretty close to just that, a Ponzi scheme of gigantic proportions. It may not surprise you to know that Bernie is not the first and will not be the last; he is only among those who have been caught. Given that most of the sophisticated money changers are stealing from unsophisticated investors on a daily basis I am a little surprised they even put him in jail. It was more who he stole from that got him thrown in jail; his client list were very large and sophisticated investors. So if you are a small unsophisticated investor you may find it amusing that they do not only steal from you, they steal from each other as well.

There is a tendency in the financial industry to almost continuously introduce new investment instruments. It is one way to continually raise the complexity that limits the opportunity for unsophisticated investors. Access to many of these designer investments is very limited even though the impact on the market overall can be significant. So while the unsophisticated are trading stock, the sophisticated can take from them by trading something other than the stock that simply impacts the stock price. We have moved too far from the buttonwood tree as the industry has fallen off the curbstone into the sewer.

I am just going to bore you with the discussion of one of these fancy financial instruments to demonstrate what has happened to the stock market the last few decades. Exchange Traded Funds (ETFs) are traded everyday on the NYSE. These are funds that do not actually own stock in any of the corporations that are part of the fund like a mutual fund does. A mutual fund actually owns the stocks in the fund and that is why they are only valued once a day after the markets close. If you own an ETF you do not own any stock in any company, you simply own an index – an index? What the hell is that? An index is like the DOW 30 or the S&P 500, the value of an index is calculated based on the actual values of the underlying stocks.

So here is how we make an ETF for you to buy. First we decide what we want to put in the ETF. Let's pretend that we want to include all the utility company stocks traded on the NYSE. What we do is create a value for the index based on the total value of all these stocks, the formula for doing this is somewhat complicated but the goal of the value formula is the make sure the value of the index accurately reflects what happens to the value of the stocks in the index. This value calculation becomes the value of the ETF. Then the market makes the ETF available for you to buy. If you think that utilities might do well you might choose to buy the ETF, if the ETF goes up, you win, if it goes down, you lose. What this ETF really is then, is a way for you to BET on what is going to happen to the utility stocks on the NYSE.

Now that you are in the casino let me show you around a little. One of the most significant differences between stocks and ETFs is the connection to reality. When you buy stock in a company you are buying a quantity of a LIMITED number of shares, in other words every public company has a limited number of shares available for people to buy. As one of the largest companies in the world GE has approximately ten point six (10.6) billion shares and if you buy GE you own some of these shares. This is not so with ETFs, in an ETF the shares are UNLIMITED since it is just a BET on what will happen to the *real* GE shares. Think about this, on a given day more money can change hands betting on what will happen to the real GE shares than actually changes hands buying or selling GE shares. This means that the BET on what will happen to the real GE shares may actually make the real GE shares decline. If this sounds like the tail is wagging the dog you are correct; while the high number of GE shares reduces the risk of this in GE stock it is a very real risk in other stocks. Today in the market you can even bet on volatility and if you look really hard you might even find horses or dog races in an ETF, I would not be surprised.

How did we get to this point? We got to this point because the government that was supposed to regulate the market does not have the competency or the will to actually regulate the market. It has become a free-for-all for just about any exotic financial instrument the money changers can design. The most complicated of these, derivatives, are so complicated that many of the experts do not understand how they work well enough to explain it to someone else. These overly complicated investments have done a number of very bad things; 1) it has made it difficult or impossible for the government regulators to actually regulate the market, 2) it has locked out the small investor, 3) it has created a market with an unlimited number of shares in play, 4) it has created imaginary shares that do not even exist but are traded every day, and more, and more, and more. In brief, the U.S stock market is not a stock market, it is a financial casino where billions of bets are bought and sold each day along with a few shares of real companies.

The greed in these markets is so insatiable that when reality and natural forces do not provide adequate growth, they develop their own imaginary financial products to do so. The ETFs and derivatives are a recent example of this. Back in the 1980's it was the mutual funds that provided a scheme that would increase the participation of individual investors therefore making the markets bigger. To keep our history straight, mutual funds have been around long before the 1980's, they were just not open to wider participation. So how does the sophisticated investor profit from mutual funds? Glad you asked.

The mutual funds are unsophisticated investments in the sense that they are really designed to allow small investors to pool their money and invest in a portfolio of stocks that will benefit from long term growth in the market. As mentioned earlier, the types of mutual funds in your retirement account are not designed to take advantage of downturns in the market so these funds cannot benefit from significant downturns such as the slow stock market crash of 2008 and 2009. During 2008 the more sophisticated investors changed their portfolios as the market went down. First they pulled out of the market while many small investors who could only remember what the insurance guy said about "dollar averaging" never changed their investments options. As the small investor kept putting their money into the declining market through mutual funds, the more sophisticated investors began to *short* the market, an option that is not available in your retirement account.

So while the market slowly crashed most Americans rode it to the very bottom all the while losing billions to the more sophisticated investment community. This was the largest wealth transfer in history and happened because of the deafening silence of those who might have helped. One of the problems for the small investor is that they are completely at the mercy of "the system", a system which they trusted and believed in, a belief that made many of them think that somebody was looking out for them….. not so. Even to this day there is no quality advice given to the small investor. While billions of dollars of small investor money was going into a declining market NO-ONE in the system was going to come on TV and tell you to pull out of the market…… and indeed they did not.

Millions of Americans were reading the papers, listening to the news, watching CNBC for hints as to what they should do……….. silence was largely the answer. If you were a little more sophisticated you might have picked up on a nuance or a hint but no-one was going to tell them to pull out of the market because if would have made the market fall even faster…. like a run on the bank. Some small investors managed to exchange their mutual fund investments for money market funds or government bond funds but the vast majority rode a forty to fifty percent decline into oblivion.

This crisis is going to give us an entire generation of retirees who tried to do the right thing and were ultimately burned, not by their own lack of hard work, but by a system that they trusted. This generation is facing retirement with retirement accounts that are destroyed and with a political environment that will add insult to injury by cutting their social security payments in their senior years. A generation who has seen interest rates declining for twenty years as the government has declared war on fixed income earners. As is shown in figure 7.1[21], rates have generally declined since 1990 and have been at 0.25 percent since late 2008.

Figure 7.1

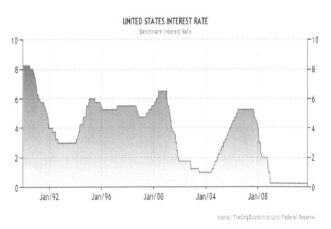

You may wonder who would benefit from a decline in interest rates, the answer is bond traders in the financial markets. When interest rates go down,

---

[21] Trading Economics.com. Federal Reserve. Available at http://www.tradingeconomics.com/united-states/interest-rate (November 2011)

bond prices go up and vice-versa. This trend has been devastating to our senior citizens who rely on fixed income investments to supplement social security and pension income. It has also been devastating on those saving for retirement since the low interest rates is part of the motivation for investing in the stock market instead, a move which has been disastrous for many nearing retirement.

The "golden years" for most of this generation will be spent working lower wage jobs throughout most of their retirement as their physical abilities and health decline…….. more like the "fools gold years". Perhaps a more devastating long-term impact of the event is the fact that their children watched this happen which has created an entire younger generation ripe with Occupy Wall Street.

In the end, the market relies on participation just like we noted in the perpetual Monopoly game example. Many average people who have participated in the stock market have experienced the Loser's Paradox and have just begun to vocalize their deep frustration. In the second half of 2011 I also see signs of the Winner's Paradox as the market looks for direction since the vast supply of Loser's have pulled out of the market and don't want to play anymore. Ultimately the market depends on wide participation and can be taken down extremely fast if vast numbers of average Americans quit playing. If vast numbers move all their retirement funds into US Treasuries instead of mutual funds, we would see the foreign ownership of our bonds go down and we would shut down the casino.

Who's own the New York Stock Exchange anyway? Well, I might as well give you one more slap in the face, of course it is not *our* market, how silly would that be. The NYSE is a corporation and another corporation, Deutsche Boerse AG, purchased sixty percent of it in February 2011 for $9.53 billion[22]. This deal created the world's largest owner of equities and derivatives markets, and the majority ownership is not even an American company. While the economy in America tanked in 2010 the NYSE (legal name NYSE Euronext) posted their second highest operating income in five years, an operating income of seven hundred and forty five million on revenue of $4.425 billion This is just the profits of the exchange, hundreds of billions are made trading by participants in the real paper chase. So you see, even when the economy is bad the market business can be very good. Understand clearly that stock markets, while they drive many countries, and the politicians and government officials tend to cater to them, they are no more part of the fabric of America or any other country than is apple pie a part of the Chinese diet.

If you really spend some time looking at the global financial system you quickly realize that this system is not constrained by national boarders, is not loyal to any particular country or nationality, and is beyond the regulatory power of every country on the planet.......

BUT,

it still relies on participation, and if the peasants..........

---

[22] Whitney Kisling, Nandini Sukumar and Elizabeth Stanton. "Deutsche Boerse's $9.53 Billion NYSE Purchase May Lead to More Takeovers", Bloomberg, Feb 15, 2011. Available at http://www.bloomberg.com/news/2011-02-15/deutsche-boerse-nyse-directors-said-to-vote-today-on-combining-exchanges.html, (October 2011).

do not participate, it will lose its grip on economies and its access to the powerful in governments. In some countries the peasants can still vote and they want to eat cake too.

Illustration 7.1

"NICE SPEECH, BUT LET'S CHANGE 'LET THEM EAT CAKE' TO 'PIE IN THE SKY.'"

8

WEALTH, CORPORATE INFLUENCE, AND GOVERNMENT ISOLATIONISM

There is a connection between institutionalized wealth created by the perpetual Monopoly game and access to corporate board rooms. As we all know institutionalized wealth is also a major player in the halls of government. If we look at how someone ends up on a corporate board we can clearly see how wealth brings access. The boards of corporations hire the CEO's and the President's and set their pay and bonus incentives. If you do not like the outrageous pay packages of these over-paid executives you should first hold the corporate boards responsible, this is who the over-paid executives are working for. So how does one end up on the board of a large corporation anyway? Well, as it turns out, in America we elect them and the election is about as fair as our typical political election. In the corporate world it is one common share = one vote so the more shares you have the more votes you have and if you have enough shares you can vote yourself on the board.

Amazing you say…. there is still more…. to make sure you get on the board you may create a voting Block, a group of individuals with relatively large stock positions in a corporation. These shareholders simply cooperate and vote all their shares for a list of candidates they want on the board (a slate), a list that is beholding to those who put them on the board. This process can be used by wealthy shareholders to take control of a corporation even though none of them own more than a fraction of the company. This demonstrates clearly how wealth provides access which provides influence which provides increased wealth as depicted in Figure 8.1. By the way, a fraction of a large corporation can be worth several hundred million dollars.

Figure 8.1 - The Wealth Cycle

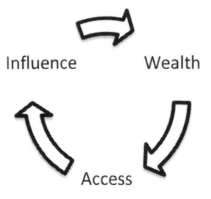

Sometimes the larger corporations are beyond the grasp of even the wealthiest of individuals and the top shares are held by other corporations instead. Today most of the top shareholders of the largest corporations are mutual funds….. yes mutual funds…. often it is the same funds you may be buying in your retirement plan. For instance the largest shareholder in GE is The Vanguard Group, Inc. which holds over 400 million shares of GE stock as of the fall of 2011 (value of these shares exceed six billion dollars). You probably own some GE stock in one of your funds right now but just don't know it. So you are thinking…. wow I own some GE stock in a mutual fund that is the largest stockholder in GE, therefore this is my voting Block, and therefore I have some influence right…… sort of.

These fund managers whom you do not even know, have the influence. These individuals belong to the same club as the members of those other voting blocks, and in fact may be part of a block themselves. The promise of mutual funds was that the little investor could have a voice, but you must realize that mutual fund managers are not compensated based on how well the fund performs, they are compensated based on how <u>big</u> the fund is. They receive a management fee which is a percentage commission based on the total size of the fund. So while the fund managers need performance to attract investment, their compensation is based on mass.

If the individuals who invest in these funds reduce their investment in the fund, the mutual fund MUST reduce their holdings of the underlying stock or re-balance the fund. So if enough peasants sell the fund, the stock is sold, the price drops, the total investment in the fund drops and so does the fund manager commissions along with the stock option values of top executives and the wealth of board members. There is an avenue for significant influence through mutual funds held by the peasants, block selling by the peasants would get every ones attention and fast. The problem with the peasants is that they just can't get organized. I can see the headline now "Peasants raid corporations by block selling of mutual funds".

Am I recommending this, actually no I am not. I merely want all peasants to understand the power that we have and I think it is important for the Winner's to understand the same thing. The Winner's Paradox predicts the consequences of an unfair game, so if the winners want the game to continue they must take better care of the small guys because ultimately, the peasants can take them down, just ask King Louis VI…… history is littered with examples of the consequences of excessive greed. What we need is fairness in our system, the ability for a significant numbers to benefit, the peasant class is growing and they have been losing for too long……. it is getting hot in the kitchen.

It has been said that anyone can lose since it does not take much effort to do so. Of course the implication is that winning takes more effort than losing and this is correct. But the further implication is that if you lose you are lazy….back to our puritan work ethic. This is not true, in America and in many economies around the world today, people are losing in spite of their effort. In fact they are losing and will continue to lose in a system that is structurally designed for most to lose. We are living in a time when mankind has made the most remarkable progress except that we have not been able to create a government and financial system in which most people win. Mankind has made remarkable progress in technology, knowledge, and tolerance. We are more inter-connected than ever and for the vast majority of mankind we are at peace. It is time we make some progress in new economic thinking so that citizens of the world can enjoy the benefits of our age. We can no longer believe that the old economic models are good enough and we need to have our best minds work on new designs for government and an economic system that is more fair to more people.

The financial system, which all developed economies depend on, has gone global and is beyond the power of national governments to control. Today even governments are held hostage to this power as we clearly seen in the 2008 crash in which the United States government in a matter of days coughed up nearly a trillion dollars to "stabilize" the system. To be fair we must acknowledge that all the banks were not involved in this deal. Only the largest banks got the nod, the ones that are "too big to fail" according to some experts; the ones that are least likely to help Americans refinance their mortgages. As we all know these big banks did not loan the TARP[23] money out to people who had their mortgages foreclosed on, so what did they do with it? Some made acquisitions and others invested the TARP money and reaped handsome profits for doing so. The real tragedy of the 2008 crash was that we lost hundreds of small banks that were at least more responsive to local and regional needs. We

---

[23] Board of Governors of the Federal Reserve System. "Troubled Asset Relief Program (TARP) Information". Available at http://www.federalreserve.gov/bankinforeg/tarpinfo.htm, (November 2011).

had 140 small banks fail in 2009, another 157 fail in 2010, and more in 2011[24]. The small bank carnage from the downturn significantly reduced the competition for the largest banks and increased their powerful stranglehold on the national economy. If they were too big to fail in 2008, they are more so now, even though congress has passed legislation to supposedly see to it that TARP does not happen again.

This new legislation is simply political pandering to a public that to a large extent does not understand what happened. The real belief within government is demonstrated by the fact that by the fall of 2011 the U.S. Treasury Secretary was reported to be advising the European governments to do the same thing, a European TARP to help their largest banks.... nothing has changed after all. We must also acknowledge that all the "big" banks really did not want to take the money but were coerced into doing so to keep all banks involved and that hundreds of smaller banks took the funds also.

While the largest banks who took TARP money have now paid it back to the U.S tax payers with interest, the fact is that the big banks made money on TARP. The smaller banks who lost money invested in Fannie Mae and Freddie Mac when they were essentially nationalized by the US Government have relied on the money to make up for their losses and will have to eventually repay with interest also. In spite of the TARP funds many of the smaller banks could not

---

[24] Dave Clarke and Roberta Rampton. "U.S. closes small bank, bringing 2011 total to 26", Reuters, March 25, 2011. Available at http://www.reuters.com/article/2011/ 03/25/usa-banks-failures-idUSN2516791420110325, (October 2011).

hold on and went out of business or were absorbed by larger banks.

The TARP experience has tipped the hand of government and made us realize who is really in control here. Most governments thrive on war, what they really fear is a collapse of the financial system. The money changers really have the upper hand. Governments do their banking with them, are relying on them to hold and process currency transactions, and are convinced that without them the government would collapse....... they may be right.

Initiating change to such a powerful system is going to be very difficult. I am convinced that politicians, once they know which way the wind is clearly blowing will quickly adjust, as will most of our corporations since they ultimately want customers for their products. The toughest area for a transition to a different model of thinking will be the financial system that operates in the background most of the time but in many ways has a stranglehold on the world when it comes to change.

The largest corporations, including the large corporate banks, have significant influence on all governments in countries in which they operate. Over the last few decades we have watched in amazement the spread of corporate influence around the globe. We are amazed at the impact of global networks such as social media that allow people around the world to transmit information, even videos, globally and instantly. We see videos posted on the web from government uprisings in Syria taken by individuals, not CNN. The power of social media makes it possible for people of all languages and cultures, even the peasants, to share information and concerns. This social network is growing fast and transcends national governments and their ability to control information. The world sees firsthand what is going on without the government filters that organized media outlets provide. But like all good things, there is a downside, and globalization has a downside.

Globalization has significantly changed the ability of governments to control large corporations as they now transcend national boarders in a global web of activity beyond the reach of any single government. To the extent that the super-wealthy have influence on these large corporations, their influence is now global also. The power of the large global corporations and the financiers that control them has created a global quasi- governmental system that is not a government at all, an elite group who have access to all governments. It is no surprise then when you see what you think are "American" corporations doing very un-American things…. don't they care about their home country anymore? Actually, they have no home country in a traditional sense as they have become inter-twined in many governments and cultures around the world. They are not American, or Chinese, or European…… they are a group interested in and very successful at economic activity and are driven to transcend national borders in order to sell their products.

They are the science fiction version of Marco Polo and you have to admire their ability to infiltrate countries that our state department still has not figured out. They have figured out how to transcend governmental systems and culture in an effort to sell more of their products. We should be so lucky to have governments capable of the same thing. If we really wanted to undermine the Taliban in Afghanistan we should have sent in McDonalds, Pepsi, and some other large US based corporations, they could have taken them down with marketing and cultural contamination a lot faster and without any loss of life.

A big problem with governments is that they trade on isolation. Their identity is based on the isolation of one people and culture, from another people and culture. In a way these large corporations are doing a great service around the world. They are the ambassadors of culture in many respects since the first taste of Western philosophy in many non-democratic countries around the world has been a can of Coke or a McDonald's hamburger. While these are probably not your favorite food groups, the introduction of these products has started a cultural conversation in many places around the globe and reinforced what many of us knew all along, people around the world are a lot more similar than their governments would indicate. All people basically want and need similar things, it is the governments that keep the people and their cultures segregated.

Having given some kudos for spreading cultural wealth we have to acknowledge that this has come at a cost to all of us. Large global corporations have become extremely powerful and influential and in some instances have used that power to undermine the same progress they have provided. The global corporations are economic machines that are interested in selling more products. They are not necessarily interested in fair competition and their appetite for accumulating control of more and more of the world commerce is never ending and ultimately gives them abusive powers. The large financial corporations have the ability to influence their home governments and even hold them hostage (too big to fail). To the extent that they cooperate, their financial power transcends national borders and provides a global platform to control and influence many different countries as a group.

In many ways large corporations have become stronger than governments. Of course governments could break up these big banks at the national level if they wanted to. It would seem that you would break them up just so the smaller banks would have a better chance of surviving but today governments are not doing this because some think that our largest national banks need to compete with the largest national banks of other countries……really? In other words our banks need to compete on a global scale….perhaps we should think this one through again. Should we have corporations that are stronger and more powerful than governments?

9

WHERE HAS ALL THIS GOTTEN US?

Most of us have played the traditional Monopoly game and have some memories about that experience. Like any board game if you liked it, played it a lot, you really enjoyed the game and probably played it more often, especially if you won enough to keep you interested. Whether or not we realize it we have also been playing the perpetual Monopoly game, but unlike the traditional game, the perpetual game is built into our lives, at least in Western economies. The perpetual game is a reflection of our economy and how it plays out for most of Americans and Europeans. Just like our new rule in the perpetual game, playing the "real life" Monopoly game is mandatory, it is built into our lives through the legal, political, and economic system which governs our behaviors and opportunities. It plays itself out over and over in our daily lives and in our modern world. The role of government is so intense that it has become more and more difficult to insulate ourselves from the game.

Just like the example demonstrated, when you are in a perpetual Monopoly game, the game is never reset and once you win you have an institutionalized advantage. In America, when you become wealthy, the system supports your ability to stay wealthy. Your access to political influence, the power of our financial system, better investment options and advice, lower risk opportunities, and experts of all types insure that you have ample opportunity to stay a winner. To a large extent wealth in America has become institutionalized bringing with it influence, access, privilege, and perpetuity. This is a generalization and does not apply to every person who becomes wealthy since it is obviously possible to lose your wealth by not taking advantage of the access that your wealth provides. However, any professional investment advisor will tell you that a person who becomes wealthy in our system should be able to maintain wealth and sustain it for future generations.

While capitalism has served us well in America, the institutionalized wealth it ultimately produced has created a modern day version of the feudal system model. Whether we intended to do so or not is a matter of debate. Just like in the feudal system of medieval Europe, the modern day Lords pass the privileges on to the next generation of heirs and the winners are sustained while the middle class disappears and more and more we look like a feudal society. Just like in the feudal era, from time to time a new lord rises up and conquers some of the old wealth but then the stability of the system quickly returns and generational privilege continues. Capitalism created the middle class and now is destroying it; pushing the middle classes into the lower classes. We are left with a modern day peasant class that are taking crumbs from the masters table (government handouts) in order to survive just like in the feudal era. Approximately forty two million Americans were on food stamps by the end of 2010 and there are even more now. Economic mobility is at a dismal four percent while unemployment is the highest level in decades. Their prospects for significantly better futures cannot be found in the eight to ten dollar an hour jobs they are likely to get when they finally get one. Is capitalism simply the latest scheme which allows the truly advantaged to maintain their advantage? Is it simply the newest way of making sure that the privileged among us are forever privileged? Is it just a new version of the feudal system? These are questions for all Americans, I am quite certain that the debate has already begun.

Of this I am fairly certain, it would be a mistake to look at our system of capitalism as merely the attempt of an advantaged class to maintain advantage. Looking at the humble beginnings of our economic system, it certainly appeared to have more to offer especially in the sense of fairness and opportunity. Unfortunately for many Americans today, the prospects and opportunities are fading, and a restlessness that we have not seen to this point in our history is emerging. Do we have the wrong system or is the system simply broken? In the fall of 2011 we watched the government incrementally tweak our system to try to encourage job growth, encourage banks to lend, encourage corporations to hire people, spend their profits…. anything that will get the tax machine running again. As the great recession of 2008 dragged on the politicians desperately tried to blame each other, banks, corporations, even the government of which they are a part….. anything but themselves.

One can hardly miss the fact that capitalism seems to be gaining ground around the world, especially in economies which were previously socialist. This begs the question – What are our choices? Do we simply have to choose between capitalism or socialism? - or some perversion of either? Can we imagine another option? When we look around the world today we see the older capitalistic or market economies under-performing in comparison to others which are not capitalistic at all. Our observation is that the old capitalistic countries experienced a zenith in their history and are now in decline. They seem to have problems with economic growth, job creation, and the best economic opportunity they present is making foreign investments in countries which are under-developed, economically disadvantaged or down right socialist or even communist…. What is really going on?

Look at Europe and the malaise that has set in post WWII. Slow growth, chronic unemployment, and lack of opportunity for the masses. This has produced a governmental system that has resorted to institutionalized welfare treatment of the peasants who are caught in a system in which they cannot escape and cannot succeed. Are we not becoming Europe?

The American model seems to be having problems as well. The growing wealth gap and annihilation of the middle class has left many families and individuals struggling for economic identity in a system which does not seem to be working for them, and indeed seems to be structurally positioned against their advance. For quite a while America has lived off borrowing against future generations to purchase more of the cheap imported goods that make some in the lower class feel like their standard of living has increased because they can afford to own ten pairs of cheap shoes, and so much cheap clothing that we don't even bother replacing a button anymore. Why should we, it is cheaper to just replace the shirt. It is rather comical that our version of capitalism in America has bought into a commodity world which is 180 degrees at odds with our capitalistic sense of wastefulness. One of the great tenets of capitalism is the efficient allocation of resources…….. this is now bringing us a mountain of eight dollar t-shirts? I must be missing the point here…. what is so efficient about waste?

To our great surprise, the newer communist/market economies like China are the stars today. One of the unintended consequences of the end of the cold war is that the relentless economic power of China was been unleashed on our consumer economy. Driven by cheap labor, a command economy that produces a five year economic plan, an ambitious under-class, and a surplus of Western consumers interested in cheap goods, especially since their standard of living is eroding; China stands to do well for some time to come. In the fall of 2011, I heard the most amazing discussion among the talking heads of CNBC, they were actually discussing the benefits of a planned economy and the five year plan of China as if it was some kind of economic revelation. I remember being a student in the 1970's and hearing in my government class about the evils of these same planned economies and how they are representative of systems in which people are not free, systems in which the government runs everything including the economy. It is amazing how much we capitalists have learned in just a few decades.

It is now a presumption of most Westerners that the rise of China will replace America as the most powerful country economically within a generation. An economic war that will eventually undo the Western war machine as the money to fund technology and modern weapons dries up and is re-allocated to fund the social security trust fund that our irresponsible politicians have been stealing from for decades. Who cares about weapons anyway, in the long run economic power is the real war machine. As we watch this played out, no one in the media seems to put much thought into what this means for capitalism as an economic model, and NO ONE dares to suggest that perhaps we are stuck in an economic model that is not competitive, a system which is not just out of fashion, but a system that is broken; the failure of capitalism.

The first people that you would think would be concerned about the failure of capitalism are those who have benefited from it most, but there is a strange silence in America. No-one is really saying much up to now. We have a few of the super-rich like Mr. Buffet offering to pay more taxes which is generous enough, but where is the outcry among our perpetual winners as a group. I would propose that we are once again witnessing a replay of what has already happened in parts of Europe. When capitalism is not working anymore, those who have benefited most are likely to resist significant change since it may very well change their advantage. If we accidently reset the perpetual Monopoly game while we are trying to fix it the result could be disastrous for this group. It is better for this group to ride it out as long as possible, use their resources to prop up a failing system, try to make it last as long as possible, and hope for the best.

So who is the change agent? Steve Jobs once commented in a commencement address[25] to Stanford students that "death was the real change agent" as it "swept away the old and made room for the young". It is my presumption, like most who heard it, that Mr. Jobs was speaking about the creative juices that drive technology development, and was suggesting that nothing but death could neutralize the influence of the institutionalized godfathers of technology who may slow down progress. These are the winners of the technology version of the perpetual Monopoly game. I think the statement may have been more intuitive than originally intended. I see the power and influence of those who are winning in a system as being the natural anti-change agents and the only way you make progress is to figure out how to reset the game or wait for "nature to take its course". The problem with the perpetual Monopoly game is that it is far more insidious than the technology version that Mr. Jobs was talking about, in perpetual Monopoly winning is not limited by mother nature as privilege is passed from one generation to the next.

There is another way to look at China and this view is the one that I think is held by many that are careful observers of capitalism in the West. This view looks at China through a historic lens, it looks into the future based on our own experiences in the West to see China also reaching a zenith; it is just a matter of time

---

[25] Transcript of Commencement Speech at Stanford given by Steve Jobs, June 14, 2005. Steve Jobs Posted on Tuesday, June 14, 2005 7:18:09 PM by Swordmaker. Available at http://www.freerepublic.com/focus/chat/1422863/posts (November 2011).

before the cycle repeats itself. Is it just a matter of where China is on the life cycle of market driven economic systems? Will they too begin to decline like Europe and America? Will it even happen faster to China in a world that seems to be moving at an ever-accelerating rate of change?

How confusing is our world.... In developed countries we basically have two governmental systems and two economic systems. We have democratic and communist governments and we have capitalistic and socialistic policies. America is holding on with a democratic government and capitalistic policies which are becoming more socialistic. Europe is holding on with democratic governments and socialistic policies, and then we have China. China is outperforming both America and Europe with a communist government and capitalistic policies. Most Americans thought that capitalism and democracy went together – what happened? The definition of capitalism according to Webster is

" an economic system characterized by private or corporate ownership of capital goods, by investments that are determined by private decision, and by prices, production, and the distribution of goods that are determined mainly by competition in a free market"

As you can see, the word democracy is not in there anywhere.... Look as you may you will find only lose connections between the two, the most significant of which is the fact that in our modern time, the countries who have supported capitalism have been largely democratic. The short history of capitalism can be found on Wikipedia[26] and may well be worth a little reading. Born on the heels of mercantilism, capitalism dates back to the Netherlands in the early 1600s producing the first "market" crash in tulip bulb trading caused by the Tulip Mania in 1636-37 in which the prices of tulips were bid up to completely irrational levels which then collapsed.......sound familiar?

Most Americans are only familiar with Industrial Capitalism based on the work of Adam Smith and others in the mid-1700s whose book "An Inquiry into the Nature and Causes of the Wealth of Nations" (shortened to The Wealth of Nations) in 1776 challenged the common belief that there was a finite amount of wealth in the world. Smith and others argued that this assumption, called absolutism was not true and suggested instead the idea that wealth can be created. Ultimately the concept of laissez-faire (meaning hands off) was popularized in the mid-1800s and added to the American model. Laissez-faire suggests that governments should not interfere with transactions between private parties (i.e. markets).

In the last half of the 1900s, especially in the 80s and 90s Financial Capitalism (sometimes referred to as Financialization) became a major force in America and around the world. This system favors financial leverage over the traditional means of producing wealth. Financialization[27] is defined by Wikipedia as

"an economic system or process that attempts to reduce all value that is exchanged (whether tangible,

---

[26] Wikipedia. "History of Capitalism". Available at http://en.wikipedia.org/wiki/History_of_capitalism, (October 2011).
[27] Wikipedia. "Financialization". Available at http://en.wikipedia.org/wiki/Financialization, (October 2011).

intangible, future or present promises, etc.) either into a financial instrument or a derivative of a financial instrument."

The Wikipedia definition is a combination of several suggested definitions being argued by academics writing in this area. In his 2006 book "American Theocracy: The Peril and Politics of Radical Religion, Oil, and Borrowed Money in the 21st Century", Kevin Phillips defined financialization as

"a process whereby financial services, broadly construed, take over the dominant economic, cultural, and political role in a national economy."[28]

After the last few years I think it is safe to substitute the word global in place of "national". Philips goes on to compare the evolution of the U.S. economy to that of Habsburg Spain in the 16th century, the Dutch trading empire in the 18th century, and the British Empire in the 19th century, a process which ended in collapse. This evolution progressed through several stages prior to collapse including in order of occurrence; "agriculture, fishing, and the like, next commerce and industry, and finally finance".

The following chart (Figure 9.1) shows the percent of our Gross domestic Product in America from the financial industry. As you can see we are approaching ten percent by 2006.

---

[28] Kevin Phillips. "American Theocracy: The Peril and Politics of Radical Religion, Oil, and Borrowed Money in the 21st Century". New York: Viking, 2006, page 268.

Figure 9.1

Financialization may really be what those protesters on Wall Street are really frustrated about. The feeling in America and much of Europe is that the corporate financial industry is destroying our world, at least the one we want to live in. From global influence on governments, to corporations and individuals, this system has a major influence on what will be produced, who will produce it, where it will be produced and how much profit will be made. This system seeks to extract a significant amount of the profits out of transactions without producing anything more than a complicated control system and the ability to maintain the smoke screen that convinces governments, corporations, and individuals that they are indispensable – this may be the ultimate Ponzi scheme. As our manufacturing jobs have declined in America, the financial system has blossomed. The America that use to make things has become an empty shell of mostly low-end service jobs……

<u>Who cares what the unemployment rate is when you can't support yourself even with a job.</u>

It is not whether or not you have a job it is more like how many jobs do you have to have for most Americans. When we get the unemployment rate down and people still cannot survive I guess we will just start publishing a second Job Unemployment rate. I must say, that this is not the small problem that many think that it is. All over the United States and in many places in Europe the peasants are losing in record numbers, even the ones who played the game well.

10

WHAT ARE THE OPTIONS?

*A*s I look at my comments in the previous chapters they seem strange to have come from me. I am a person who played the game, has won a little, and am institutionalized in a small way in our perpetual Monopoly game. Being a white male I have had some advantage which was somewhat neutralized by my parents lack of education and economic resources. I would say that good fortune, good mentors, hard work, and a gracious God (are we allowed to say that anymore?) are my reasons for having had such a good ride so far. I also credit our system that still rewards SOME, myself included, who have played by the rules. Unfortunately for far too many it has not worked out so well.

Have I become the revolutionary? Am I calling for the over-throw of governments? Am I no longer a believer in the system? In the preface to this book I raised several possibilities of how people will evaluate me as an author of such a potentially controversial book with such controversial analogies and statements. I still do not know how these questions will be answered by others but for my part I maintain that my life experiences and observations have led me to these conclusions. My experience in small business had a great influence on me. In small businesses you typically know your employees and you are also more aware of what is going on in their lives. In many ways my employees reminded me of my own children and my role as a parent. As a parent you always want to see your children win. Just like my mythical aunt example and the checkers game, I felt obligated to create situations in which everyone could win. The first rule about this is that everyone does not want to win, or at least everyone does not define winning the same way. As a young manager I often made the mistake of thinking that my trek through life, my version of success, is what everyone wanted, I could not have been more wrong.

I remember as a manager, encouraging a single mother to go to school so I could promote her to a position that paid more money which I translated into better economic security for her and her daughter. For years she resisted, she even told me once that she did not want to move into management because she would inherit an expanding backside from setting at a desk all day. Years later, when she did end up in management, I discovered that the real story was she did not want to take time away from her daughter to either go to school or move into management; a job that involved less regular hours. She also had reservations about going back to school given that her high school experience wasn't exactly memorable. At every turn I have made the wrong assumptions about what success means, and at this point in my life I profess to know just a bit more than I did then. The one thing that I do know is that the perception of fairness looms large in people everywhere, not just in America and to a great extent it is the most important concept of any economic system.

My apologies to those who had other expectations but this book is not inciting revolution in any way, it is simply an attempt to raise the questions that we all need to answer in Western capitalistic systems. If the system is not working anymore, let's admit it and start talking about ways in which we can change things. Change does not have to happen through revolution, it can happen through transformation. The burning question is - how do we re-configure ourselves without stopping the game? Stopping the game would have grave consequences for all and could lead to the collapse of several Western economies and set Asia back at least 30 years. Re-thinking our way into the future will not happen if we merely attempt to make incremental changes to our system. We have been trying that for a while to no avail – no, we are at a point in which we need radical change. We are at a point in which we have to consider re-thinking our economics and how we count things, how we value things, and how we allocate things. How can this be accomplished without causing system failure? What changes should we make? ....and when?

The closest we have ever come to resetting the perpetual Monopoly in America was probably the Great Depression. The wealth accumulation of many prior generations was slashed causing some of those that were in the market extreme losses that could never be recovered. We must remember though that not all wealth, or even most of the wealth was in the market when it fell and virtually none of the lower classes were in the market at all. We also must remember that the wealthy that were heavy in the stock market were not the only ones suffering extreme hardship as an entire generation of the lower classes took the brunt of the hit. This lends some credibility to the statement that when you aim for the big guy you often hit the small guy. This is a statement that is worth noting as we consider alternatives.

Besides the Great Depression probably the closest we have come to collapse is the economic crisis that began in 2008. We all have lived through this so there is no point in recounting the history. As in prior crises, the arguments over the causes will continue for some time. Some will say that we should have let the banks fail, the stock market crash, and the government default. Others will blame politicians, some will blame banks, some will blame corporations, the investment community (Wall Street), or even China. No one seems too anxious to blame our economic model.

We know that economies such as ours go through cycles and from time to time will go through a recession (boom and bust cycle), a kind of miniature version of restarting the Monopoly game. In an attempt to keep 1929 from ever happening again, we have borrowed our way out of the last few cycles; in fact we have done all kinds of things to see to that we never come so close again, ironically this only slowed the 2008 crash and did not prevent it. Some experts maintain that it is in all of our best interest to prevent the type of economic event that would reset the game but I am not so sure. The argument continues. From a perpetual Monopoly game point of view the institutionalized winners should intervene to hold their position and avoid a collapse. The collapse would have of course been a disaster for some, but it would have created opportunity for others. Often after a collapse it is the institutionalized wealth that benefits most. When you consider the housing crash in 2009 and 2010 you must realize that this created great opportunities for those who had money to invest. Purchasing foreclosed and under-valued properties that will generate handsome profits as real estate recovers. This is part of the "win-win" cycle that economic resources provide to take advantage of the "lose-lose" cycle of most of Americans. The winners in the game also win when things go bad and the losers just keep on losing.

Before I say much more I will disqualify myself as an expert economist because I am not. I will add however, in some instances, I think being an expert is a disadvantage. Having a capitalistic economist tell you what is wrong with a capitalistic economy is similar to asking a communist socialist to identify the disadvantages of socialism. They will always try to respond within the constraints of the system which limits their ability to see things from a fresh perspective. We call this a paradigm problem. Your paradigm[29] is like the lens through which you see things, we are limited by what we have been exposed to and therefore have a problem with seeing things from a fresh perspective. As a professor, I always tell my students that the good news is that education will expand their

---

[24] Definition of a paradigm: par•a•digm/ˈparəˌdīm/ noun: 1. A typical example or pattern of something; a model. 2. A worldview underlying the theories and methodology of a particular scientific subject.

minds and enable them to see the world differently, but the bad news is that it will also limit what they can see. Knowledge is a double-edged sword, on the one hand it expands our mind but on the other it limits our ability to interpret things or see things clearly. Knowledge contaminates these abilities because it teaches us how to think, a process to follow, which drives our mental processes, and our view of the world. It serves us well most of the time but can fail us when it comes to the simplest things in life. Like the common saying... we often suffer from drinking our own Kool-Aid. I certainly do not exempt myself in any way from this limitation as I try to ask some important questions about our economic future on the small blue planet.

The economy is something most of us know little about even though we feel its impact on us every day. Like the story about an employee who wanted a raise. When the employee went to his boss to ask for a raise the boss began complaining about the economy and asked the employee if he understood how bad the economic conditions were. The employee then told the boss, I am not an expert on the economy but I am an expert on my economy, and my resident expert, my wife says we are not doing to good right now. As a person who has participated and has paid pretty close attention, I am also an expert on what I have seen and experienced.

The Loser's Paradox predicts the outcome of losing excessively. Here is a list of things that send the message to most Americans that they are losing excessively

1. The wealth gap that overwhelmingly favors a small group has grown dramatically in recent decades.
2. The income gap that is growing and destroying the middle class.
3. Use of American tax payer dollars to Bail out large corporations and banks, in some cases, the same ones that are held responsible for the last collapse in 2008.
4. <u>No</u> use of American tax payer dollars to bail out average Americans when their home values were upside down.
5. Foreclosure on millions of homes with nothing but an empty promise and a strange silence from government.
6. Flat incomes at the lower end of the earning scale while the upper end continues to grow.
7. Devastated retirement and savings accounts caused by the last financial downturn which produced the largest wealth transfer in history from the losers to the winners.
8. A government that has declared war on the elderly by following economic policies that intentionally keep interest rates near zero, destroying safe interest income havens such as CD's.
9. Gloomy future outlook, stagnation, and the understanding that the average American will be the last to benefit when things get better. Some to most will never recover.
10. High unemployment and the best solution some in government can offer is to borrow more money from China to hire more government employees.

11. Constantly being told that they can only be helped if we help those who are suffering the least (i.e. large corporations, low taxes on wealth and the wealthy).
12. The flat and inverted economic mobility lines that clearly show that the probability to improve your lot in life is a dismal four percent in America contrary to the promise of our democracy.
13. The greater access and influence of those with tremendous wealth to the benefits of America.
14. A stock market system which is structurally designed to take advantage of the small investor and the apparent cooperation between the government, the wealthy, and the market to keep it that way.
15. The feeling that they are trapped into participating in a system they no longer support.

I am convinced that this list is incomplete since every time I spend more time on it I find that I left something out. I am sure that you can add a few of your own suggestions if you really think about it. It is no surprise that those who are losing in our governmental and economic system feel rather hopeless and that is a very bad sign. As I said before, the wonders of democracy, and the wonders of the one person one vote make it possible for things to change, and things can change really fast.

Remember the Loser's Paradox and the three phases? Phase one is <u>losing excessively</u>.... well most of the population in America and Europe is certainly feeling this. Phase two is <u>the desire not to play</u> and most people are way past that as well; they just don't know how to quit. Phase three is <u>the realization that if they stop playing that they cannot win</u>, resulting in the paradox. Most people are at phase three in this progression. Some have quit already. We have a younger generation that does not really believe they can win after watching their parents so they pretty much quit before they ever started. This is a group that has run up record student loan debt to build skills for jobs that don't exist. If you think about it, this is also a wealth transfer. But most Americans still have not given up on winning but we are losing more and more of us

Illustration 10.1

"I'm sorry that some of you are starving to death, but we *all* have to make sacrifices."

every day. The third phase of the Loser's Paradox has two possible outcomes based on what the loser believes about the future. Either the loser believes that they can win so they keep playing, or they give up on winning and quit. When those who are losing quit they not only give up on winning but they give up on the game itself. No government cheerleading can substitute for legitimate opportunity.

I would predict that this is the seed for real social unrest of people all over the world, in particular America and Europe. Unless we can create a more fair system, a system that will still have winners and losers, but a system where the differences are not so dramatic, we are going to see more and more upheaval in what we consider the "developed" countries of the world. We also have to realize that people's lives are enhanced by doing meaningful work[30] for what they consider a fair wage. It simply is not true that the peasants, as a group, are lazy and do not want to work. There is a lot of good science on this if you want to investigate it further[31].

---

[30] Also referred to as "worthwhile work".
[31] CHA. "Worthwhile work: A CHA report", CHA the Workplace Communication Consultancy, Spring 2008. Available at http://zookri.com/Portals/6/reports/ worthwhile%20work.pdf, (October 2011).

11

THE SOLUTION TO THE LOSER'S PARADOX

When we look back to our earlier discussion of the perpetual Monopoly game we came up with two natural consequences of the game. I am restating them here for purposes of laying the foundation for the conclusion. Remember that after losing excessively, the loser begins to experience a negative response to the game (phase 1). This results in a desire to quit playing (phase 2). Finally the Loser realizes that if they quit the game they can never win (phase 3). The consequences of the Loser's Paradox are summed up in the following series of statements:

When a player has lost excessively, their desire not to lose is greater than their belief that they can win so they do not play the game.

Desire not to lose > Belief that they can win   does not play

When a player's desire not to lose is equal to their belief they can win then they are indifferent toward playing the game

Desire not to lose = Belief that they can win   indifferent to play

When a player's desire not to lose is less than their belief they can win they are going to resume playing the game

Desire not to lose < Belief that they can win   play resumes

On the other hand, the Winner's Paradox is the result of winning excessively through skill, privilege, or luck. The first phase of this is winning excessively. The second phase is nobody wants to play with the winner anymore and the third phase is that the winner realizes that if they want the game to go on they must help others win. The consequences of the Winner's Paradox are summed up in the following series of statements:

When the desire to win is greater than their desire to help others win as well, the winner will want to play but there will no one to play with and the play will stop

Desire to win > Desire to help others win as well   play stops

When the desire to win is equal to the desire to help others win as well the winner is indifferent about playing

Desire to win = Desire to help others win as well   indifference to play

When the desire to win is less than the desire to help others win as well, play resumes

Desire to win < Desire to help others win as well   play resumes

The basic concern in the solution is what combination will insure that the game will continue to be played. Since the perpetual Monopoly game is a proxy for our real economy the end of the game means that the economy collapses. We need to find some balance between these two and we can start by looking at two things we learned from analyzing the dynamics of winning and losing in our imaginary game. With the Loser we realized that the pivotal decision was based on what the Loser believed about their prospects of winning in the future. In other words, it is important for the Loser to believe that the game is fair. We also realized that the pivotal decision for the Winner was based on their willingness to help others win. The Winner will decide this based on their desire for participation which is required for play to continue. Combining these two statements we come up with the following equilibrium.

Let W_d = winners desire for participation and L_p = losers perception regarding fairness

When these are in some approximate equilibrium we have a stable economic system based on cooperation.

$W_d \sim L_p$ <u>cooperation</u>

Without some balance between the Winner's desire for participation and Losers perception of fairness the game is over. It is important to realize that the ultimate responsibility for whether or not the game continues is primarily up to the Winner. In fact the Winner must convince the Loser that the game is fair. In economies all over the world there are winners and losers and the equation is exactly the same. I originally happened on this concept in a small business environment in which I noticed the unfortunate pattern of losing. In life it seems that most of us are destined to lose unless somewhere along the way we find a compassionate winner, I have had several in my life, and they kept me in the game at critical times. I also realized the power of winning which is the power to help someone else win. There is nothing like winning, and helping others win is almost as satisfying as winning yourself..... I am sure you have experienced this with your children if you are a parent.

All over the world people are losing and I for one feel like the clock is ticking. It is only a matter of time before the pot boils over. As I have written this book I have had to challenge myself on what I believe and why, I have had to ask myself some tough questions about things that I have experienced and things that I have learned. In the end I had to define things about my beliefs that I really never had answers to. Like other writing I have done, I found the process to be very reflective. Since I raised the possibilities of how others may view me based on this work I will give you my reflections here.

As it turns out I am not anti-government, I really don't think anybody is. I think we can become anti our government and I am not that either. I think that

America has been a great experience in government that has captured the attention of the world for good reason. We have the most diverse society of any country in the world and while we have made huge mistakes and inflicted significant harm, on the whole we have done well, there are many despots around the world available for rational hating. Having made this basic statement I think we are at a fork in the road along with other Western European countries. We have a lot of unhappy people in our country and we simply cannot ignore that or explain it away in jest. One thing that I do believe is this – we can fail.

I am not anti-business or anti-corporation. I think corporations are like people, they have a personality and some of them are nice to know and do very good things. Others are takers and pure winners in that they will sacrifice the game rather than moderate their greed. You can easily think of some corporations that are the good guys as well as the bad guys. More and more I find myself looking at some of our financial corporations as very bad actors in our system and the best example of the pure winner that I can think of. We must find a way to reel in the money changers who are pushing us into <u>financial capitalism</u> on a global scale.

This is the single most identifiable threat to our future in my opinion. This group are takers not producers, and in many ways they are bad for our economy, and they are bad for the global economy. By the way, for our European friends, the largest number of Financialism (financial capitalism) transactions are produced from London not New York. This group has replaced the lost profits of legitimate production with the attempt to control production and extract profits based on a system that they designed and then convinced and coerced others to play. They do not mind the fact that their home countries are empty shells of their former selves as they seek to reduce every aspect of existence to a financial transaction.

Even though I have some serious issues with the way our current markets are run I am not anti-stock market either, I have traded since the late 80s and I see the potential of a fair market based on some simple concepts. One of these concepts is the social benefit derived from average citizens investing in their public corporations and benefiting from the increase in value. This is potentially a great symbiotic win-win relationship that I think most Americans understand. What has happened to our stock market is that it has been hijacked by the financial capitalists and turned into a casino in which the odds are overwhelmingly favoring the house. In addition they have hijacked the basic human desire to win and used it to conduct hi-tech Ponzi schemes with complicated financial instruments that have stolen many multiples of the $50 billion that Bernie Madoff took. Worse yet is the influence and infiltration of their members and their philosophers in the ranks of government that have reinforced the legitimacy of an illegitimate system. They have tried to make everyone, including the government believe that the way to help the "little guy" is to let the "big guy" have more. This could actually work if we were talking about "big guys" who were actually producing something but this is not the case with the financial capitalists, they are pure takers. A "big guy" with an ounce of benevolence can do a lot of good. This led to the bad decision to help the big banks at the expense of the 297 small banks that failed in 2009 and 2010, banks that were much more likely to help the communities they lived in. The choice to help the banks was also made at the expense of Americans who could have had their mortgages restructured directly by the government through the banks which they regulate. This is a historically bad decision. How is it that we could have a government that will help a few large financial corporations with the money of American tax payers rather than extend the help to those who paid the taxes in the first place? This decision will live in infamy and will be the rallying call of a generation against the institutions and individuals who made this decision. We are only beginning to see the consequences of this massive error. In a tax system that relies on voluntary compliance the government is playing roulette. Without the <u>participation</u> of the American taxpayer there is no bailout.

In the end I can honestly say that winning and losing are both good. I have learned the most when I lost, in fact through losing I learned how to win. It took me much longer to learn the real value of winning. I know now that the real value of winning is that it qualifies you to help others win as well. As a small business owner and as a professor of business I have had the wonderful experience of helping and watching people win, many without my help.

12

THE AGE OF COOPERATION

We are entering what I would call the Age of Cooperation. This will be a time in which the survival and prosperity of humanity will depend on cooperation, rather than self-interest and capitalistic competition. The Age of Cooperation will eventually see the decline and extinction of both capitalism and socialism, it will see the rise of humanity which will cooperate globally for the benefit of humanity. As our little blue planet becomes figuratively smaller, the interdependence of all of us has become obvious. It is no longer possible for individuals or governments to isolate themselves from this reality. The financial system and other large corporations were the first to realize that global cooperation was the only option. The rest of us are not far behind.

We can foresee the day when many average Americans will follow in the footsteps of the wealthy, the global corporations, and financial system. A day when the benefits of being American or being in America are marginalized by the elimination of barriers to freedom of movement on a global scale. Many Americans already move about the globe without political risk and the fear of isolation with the aid of modern technology that keep us connected and the trend toward peaceful coexistence on a figuratively shrinking planet. How long will it be before governments have to compete for their citizenry? How long will it be before the peasants escape the controlling mechanisms of nation-based governmental and economic systems and choose where they live, work, and play?

For many Americans it is a small step to go abroad when their opportunities are grim and their future is unknown at home. Do they stay in the game with a corrupt dysfunctional government and broken economic system or look for a better place to go? It used to be that average Americans never considered living elsewhere but this is changing as the benefits from staying in America are marginalized by the benefits of living abroad. The Age of Cooperation will marginalize the role of government as the need for collaboration supersedes the benefits of isolation.

Like any new age, this new age will come into existence either by a process of transformation or revolution, the choice is ours. At this time some of us have more power than others, and it is up to us to see to it that this is a transformative process not one that is born of destruction. We must first embrace its inevitability and the consequences of revolt. We must acknowledge that too many citizen peasants on the little blue planet have been losing too much, too often, and for too long.

Globalization of corporations and the financial system has not happened in a vacuum. One of the most amazing contributions of technology is the globalization of social media through the web, texting, face book, twitter, and much more. This mega-trend will have an incredible influence on our world in the near future as it has enabled global responses of people and groups we typically do not hear from such as the vast numbers of people experiencing the Loser's Paradox.

As we look around the world today we see something strange but completely predictable in the Loser's Paradox. As the perpetual Monopoly game has gone global so has the winners and losers. More and more winners around the globe are looking airily similar as do the losers. Whether it is in China, Europe, United States, Canada, South Africa, India, Japan, even Brazil, the similarities are coming into focus. Given the power of social media and the nature of inter-connectedness, this is enabling the masses to have a single, <u>and very loud</u>, voice. The world has witnessed many peasant uprisings', our next peasant uprising could very well be global. Many of those struggling in America, Europe, China, and many other countries around the world have very similar feelings related to their view of the future and their personal beliefs about their prospects for winning. Most are experiencing the Loser's Paradox and have a negative view of the future. We may just be waiting for some mega-event to light the fuse. If this were to happen the revolt would be like nothing the world has ever seen.

Almost over-night we could see vast numbers around the globe become uncontrollable by governments as the peasants quit participating. We could see institutions collapse along with governments. We could see institutionalized wealth become worthless along with the access and influence that it provides. We could see the financial system and the powerful global corporations collapse and become powerless. All these things could happen in a remarkably short period of time considering the impact and affordability of social media.

The promise of capitalism was that most people could win, i.e. the great middle class. The reality of capitalism is that the vast majority did not win. The promise of socialism was that everyone would be equal and there were to be no winners or losers. The reality of socialism is that everybody lost; even the winners were losers when compared to capitalism. I want more to win.....why can't most win? The solution to the Winner's Paradox is that the winner is compelled to help the loser enough so they will keep playing the game. None of the governmental and economic systems around the world have figured out how to do this, at least in a sustainable way. Are we to just collapse again? I hope not.

Humanity's struggle has been based on competition but all this is about to change as we move into a future in which the impact of technology and globalization will force more cooperation at the expense of competition. What kind of economic and governmental systems will support this future? It is up to us to decide. Instead of incrementalizing ourselves into oblivion we need to imagine our future world and the systems that we will need to continue human progress.

I sincerely hoped you enjoyed this read and would like to hear from you at our website. If you are interested in additional information on this and other associated works please visit www.peasantsociety.com. and don't forget to join The Peasant Society of the Small Blue Planet

Glenn

APPENDIX

HAVING SOME FUN WITH MONOPOLY

Throughout this book I have used the Monopoly game to discuss our historical and current economic system to illustrate the frustration that has developed in Western democracies over recent decades. Just as I was finishing the book I awoke around 2:00 am with the idea of making up a set of rules for a Peasant version of the traditional Monopoly game. Since the peasants don't have the money to just go out and buy a special edition of the game I thought I should use the existing game, with some modification to the rules rather than call on Hasbro for a special edition. The official Monopoly game rules can be found at the Hasbro website[32] and are reproduced here exactly with

---

[32] Official Monopoly game rules from Hasbro available at http://www.hasbro.com/common/instruct/monins.pdf, (October 2011).

the exception of the misspelled word "judgement" in the official rules, hope this does not cause any confusion.

In the following paragraphs I restate the Hasbro rules for the traditional game with special rules for the Peasant version immediately following each section. The Peasant rules are in *ITALICS* for clarification. In the peasant version the peasant is setup to lose the game just like in the real world. Please feel free to modify these rules and improve upon them, when you do please post them at www.peasantsociety.com[33] so others can enjoy them. Following the section on Peasant rules I have listed some suggested rule modifications for a perpetual version of the game.

Official Monopoly rules with peasant version modifications

OBJECT... The object of the game is to become the wealthiest player through buying, renting and selling property.

PEASANT RULES – All players are peasants with the exception of the banker. Object is to be the best peasant so the person who goes out first wins. The idea is to lose because of the system not because you try to lose so in the peasant game all peasants must play with winning motivation (peasants honor). Once the first peasant is out of the game (the winning peasant) the remaining peasants can collaborate against the banker. If the peasants are able to force the banker to be saved from bankruptcy then it is considered a successful revolt and the game ends. See the rules on bankruptcy below for a full discussion.

---

[33] Affiliated with the publication of this book.

EQUIPMENT... The equipment consists of a board, 2 dice, tokens, 32 houses and 12 hotels. There are Chance and Community Chest cards, a Title Deed card for each property and play money.

PEASANT RULES– No change

PREPARATION... Place the board on a table and put the Chance and Community Chest cards face down on their allotted spaces on the board. Each player chooses one token to represent him/her while traveling around the board. Each player is given $1500 divided as follows: 2 each of $500's, $100's and $50's; 6 $20's; 5 each of $10's, $5's and $1's. All remaining money and other equipment go to the Bank.

PEASANT RULES – Banker gets the normal amount of money, the peasants get $500 less. All the players except the banker should dress like a peasant. The banker has to wear a black hat if available.

BANKER... Select as Banker a player who will also make a good Auctioneer. A Banker who plays in the game must keep his/her personal funds separate from those of the Bank. When more than five persons play, the Banker may elect to act only as Banker and Auctioneer.

PEASANT RULES – Players roll the dice to see who has to be the banker, the person with the lowest roll is the banker. The banker has two turns each round of play to one for all the peasants.

THE BANK... Besides the Bank's money, the Bank holds the Title Deed cards and houses and hotels prior to purchase and use by the players. The Bank pays salaries and bonuses. It sells and auctions properties and hands out their proper Title Deed cards; it sells houses and hotels to the players and loans money when required on mortgages. The Bank collects all taxes, fines, loans and interest, and the price of all properties which it sells and auctions. The Bank never "goes broke." If the Bank runs out of money, the Banker may issue as much more as may be needed by writing on any ordinary paper.

PEASANT RULES – The bank also collects the following additional fees. Making change - $1, sale of a property - $5, mortgage fee when you mortgage a property - $10.

THE PLAY... Starting with the Banker, each player in turn throws the dice. The player with the highest total starts the play: Place your token on the corner marked "GO," throw the dice and move your token in the direction of the arrow the number of spaces indicated by the dice. After you have completed your play, the turn passes to the left. The tokens remain on the spaces occupied and proceed from that point on the player's next turn. Two or more tokens may rest on the same space at the same time.

According to the space your token reaches, you may be entitled to buy real estate or other properties — or obliged to pay rent, pay taxes, draw a Chance or Community Chest card, "Go to Jail ®," etc.

If you throw doubles, you move your token as usual, the sum of the two dice, and are subject to any privileges or penalties pertaining to the space on which you land. Retaining the dice, throw again and move your token as before. If you throw doubles three times in succession, move your token immediately to the space marked "In Jail" (see JAIL).

PEASANT RULES – Banker takes two turns

"GO"… Each time a player's token lands on or passes over GO, whether by throwing the dice or drawing a card, the Banker pays him/her a $200 salary. The $200 is paid only once each time around the board. However, if a player passing GO on the throw of the dice lands 2 spaces beyond it on Community Chest, or 7 spaces beyond it on Chance, and draws the "Advance to GO" card, he/she collects $200 for passing GO the first time and another $200 for reaching it the second time by instructions on the card.

PEASANT RULES – Banker gets $200 for passing "GO" and the peasants get $100.

BUYING PROPERTY… Whenever you land on an un-owned property you may buy that property from the Bank at its printed price. You receive the Title Deed card showing ownership; place it face up in front of you. If you do not wish to buy the property, the Banker sells it at auction to the highest bidder. The buyer pays the Bank the amount of the bid in cash and receives the Title Deed card for that property. Any player, including the one who declined the option to buy it at the printed price, may bid. Bidding may start at any price.

PEASANT RULES – Pay a $5 fee to the bank when you buy property

<u>PAYING RENT</u>… When you land on property owned by another player, the owner collects rent from you in accordance with the list printed on its Title Deed card. If the property is mortgaged, no rent can be collected. When a property is mortgaged, its Title Deed card is placed face down in front of the owner. It is an advantage to hold all the Title Deed cards in a color-group (e.g., Boardwalk and Park Place; or Connecticut, Vermont and Oriental Avenues) because the owner may then charge double rent for unimproved properties in that color-group. This rule applies to un-mortgaged properties even if another property in that color-group is mortgaged. It is even more advantageous to have houses or hotels on properties because rents are much higher than for unimproved properties. The owner may not collect the rent if he/she fails to ask for it before the second player following throws the dice.

PEASANT RULES – Double rent is collected or paid for any owned property even if the player does not have a complete set.

<u>"CHANCE" AND "COMMUNITY CHEST"</u>… When you land on either of these spaces, take the top card from the deck indicated, follow the instructions and return the card face down to the bottom of the deck. The "Get Out of Jail Free" card is held until used and then returned to the bottom of the deck. If the player who draws it does not wish to use it, he/she may sell it, at any time, to another player at a price agreeable to both.

PEASANT RULES – Peasant does not get to keep the "Get Out of Jail Free" card. If a peasant draws the card he/she must turn it over to the banker and pay a fine of $10 to the bank. Only the banker can use the card.

"INCOME TAX"... If you land here you have two options: You may estimate your tax at $200 and pay the Bank, or you may pay 10% of your total worth to the Bank. Your total worth is all your cash on hand, printed prices of mortgaged and un-mortgaged properties and cost price of all buildings you own. You must decide which option you will take before you add up your total worth.

PEASANT RULES – Peasant pays the higher of 10% or $200, banker pays the lower of 10% or $200.

"JAIL"... You land in Jail when... (1) your token lands on the space marked "Go to Jail"; (2) you draw a card marked "Go to Jail"; or (3) you throw doubles three times in succession. When you are sent to Jail you cannot collect your $200 salary in that move since, regardless of where your token is on the board, you must move it directly into Jail. Yours turn ends when you are sent to Jail. If you are not "sent" to Jail but in the ordinary course of play land on that space, you are "Just Visiting," you incur no penalty, and you move ahead in the usual manner on your next turn. You get out of Jail by... (1) throwing doubles on any of your next three turns; if you succeed in doing this you immediately move forward the number of spaces shown by your doubles throw; even though you had thrown doubles, you do not take another turn; (2) using the "Get Out of Jail Free" card if you have it; (3) purchasing the "Get Out of Jail Free" card from another player and playing it; (4) paying a fine of $50 before you roll the dice on either of your next two turns. If you do not throw doubles by your third turn, you must pay the $50 fine. You then get out of Jail and immediately move forward the number of spaces shown by your throw. Even though you are in Jail, you may buy and sell property, buy and sell houses and hotels and collect rents.

PEASANT – The jail rules regarding "Get Out of Jail Free" card only apply to the banker.

<u>"FREE PARKING"</u>… A player landing on this place does not receive any money, property or reward of any kind. This is just a "free" resting place.

PEASANT RULES – There is no rest for the peasant so the peasants must pay a $5 loafing penalty if they land on "Free Parking". The money goes to the bank.

<u>HOUSES</u>… When you own all the properties in a color-group you may buy houses from the Bank and erect them on those properties. If you buy one house, you may put it on any one of those properties. The next house you buy must be erected on one of the unimproved properties of this or any other complete color-group you may own. The price you must pay the Bank for each house is shown on your Title Deed card for the property on which you erect the house. The owner still collects double rent from an opponent who lands on the unimproved properties of his/her complete color-group. Following the above rules, you

may buy and erect at any time as many houses as your judgment and financial standing will allow. But you must build evenly, i.e., you cannot erect more than one house on any one property of any color-group until you have built one house on every property of that group. You may then begin on the second row of houses, and so on, up to a limit of four houses to a property. For example, you cannot build three houses on one property if you have only one house on another property of that group. As you build evenly, you must also break down evenly if you sell houses back to the Bank (see SELLING PROPERTY).

PEASANT RULES – Peasants are encouraged to buy houses. The banker does not have to follow the build evenly requirement of the official rules.

HOTELS… When a player has four houses on each property of a complete color-group, he/she may buy a hotel from the Bank and erect it on any property of the color-group. He/she returns the four houses from that property to the Bank and pays the price for the hotel as shown on the Title Deed card. Only one hotel may be erected on any one property.

PEASANT RULES – The peasants are not allowed to purchase hotels since it is assumed that they cannot afford one unless they have engaged in some type of illegal activity.

BUILDING SHORTAGES… When the Bank has no houses to sell, players wishing to build must wait for some player to return or sell his/her houses to the Bank before building. If there are a limited number of houses and hotels available and two or more players wish to buy more than the Bank has, the houses or hotels must be sold at auction to the highest bidder.

PEASANT RULES – If the bank runs out of houses to sell and the banker wants to buy one, the banker can purchase a house from a peasant at one-half the value paid for the house (eminent domain). The banker then has to pay the going rate to the bank for building a house on the property.

SELLING PROPERTY... Unimproved properties, railroads and utilities (but not buildings) may be sold to any player as a private transaction for any amount the owner can get; however, no property can be sold to another player if buildings are standing on any properties of that color-group. Any buildings so located must be sold back to the Bank before the owner can sell any property of that color-group.

Houses and hotels may be sold back to the Bank at any time for one-half the price paid for them.

All houses on one color-group must be sold one by one, evenly, in reverse of the manner in which they were erected. All hotels on one color-group may be sold at once, or they may be sold one house at a time (one hotel equals five houses), evenly, in reverse of the manner in which they were erected.

PEASANT RULES – Banker gets the full value of a house when it is sold back to the bank.

MORTGAGES... Unimproved properties can be mortgaged through the Bank at any time. Before an improved property can be mortgaged, all the buildings on all the properties of its color-group must be sold back to the Bank at half price. The mortgage value is printed on each Title Deed card. No rent can be collected on mortgaged properties or utilities, but rent can be collected on un-mortgaged properties in the same group. In order to lift the mortgage, the owner must pay the Bank the amount of the mortgage plus 10% interest. When all the properties of a color-group are no longer mortgaged, the owner may begin to buy back houses at full price. The player who mortgages property retains possession of it and no other player may secure it by lifting the mortgage from the Bank. However, the owner may sell this mortgaged property to another player at any agreed price. If you are the new owner, you may lift the mortgage at once if you wish by paying off the mortgage plus 10% interest to the Bank. If the mortgage is not lifted at once, you must pay the Bank 10% interest when you buy the property and if you lift the mortgage later you must pay the Bank an additional 10% interest as well as the amount of the mortgage.

PEASANT RULES – Peasants cannot get mortgages since any property they buy immediately declines in value and is worth less than 50% of the price originally paid. Only the banker gets to mortgage properties.

BANKRUPTCY... You are declared bankrupt if you owe more than you can pay either to another player or to the Bank. If your debt is to another player, you must turn over to that player all that you have of value and retire from the game. In making this settlement, if you own houses or hotels, you must return these to the Bank in exchange for money to the extent of one-half the amount paid for them; this cash is given to the creditor. If you have mortgaged property you also turn this property over to your creditor but the new owner must at once pay the Bank the amount of interest on the loan, which is 10% of the value of the property. The new owner who does this may then, at his/her option, pay the principal or hold the property until some later turn, then lift the mortgage. If he/she holds property in this way until a later turn, he/she must pay the interest again upon lifting the mortgage. Should you owe the Bank, instead of another player, more than you can pay (because of taxes or penalties) even by selling off buildings and mortgaging property, you must turn over all assets to the Bank. In this case, the Bank immediately sells by auction all property so taken, except buildings. A bankrupt player must immediately retire from the game. The last player left in the game wins.

PEASANT RULES – The banker is not allowed to go bankrupt. If the banker is bankrupt he/she is bailed out by the peasants. If the banker owes more than they have in property and cash then the peasants are assessed a special tax to cover the amount of the deficit. This peasant tax is paid evenly by each peasant still in the game. If this happens a second time in the game, the peasants have successfully revolted and the game ends.

MISCELLANEOUS… Money can be loaned to a player only by the Bank and then only by mortgaging property. No player may borrow from or lend money to another player.

PEASANT RULES – No money is loaned to peasants by the bank.

PERPETUAL MONOPOLY

Since the perpetual Monopoly game in the book never ends I do not expect that there are many people interested in playing a board game version of real life. I gave some consideration to the rule changes necessary to play perpetual Monopoly with the traditional game set. I came up with the following modifications. You may be able to improve on these modifications with your own version. Feel free to post your recommended rules for everyone at www.peasantsociety.com. The first step in playing the perpetual Monopoly game is to borrow some additional game sets so you will have more property, money, houses etc….to last longer than the normal game. If you run out of game pieces or money you are allowed to create virtual game pieces or money similar to many of the financial instruments in the stock market (i.e. the ETF which is a virtual stock). The decision of how to do this is up to the banker.

The second modification is that players are not allowed to quit so when they are bankrupt they receive a loan from the bank to keep them in the game. This is consistent with the peasant experience of living in debt to the bank.

The third modification is that additional property sets are sold (based on the number of extra sets you have) to allow the continuous expansion of the game. Just like the vertical property development in Manhattan, perpetual Monopoly allows for the doubling and tripling of property, houses, and hotels on the same site. So a player may buy three Boardwalk properties to allow them to collect three times the normal rent from another player landing on the property. The same applies to houses and hotels.

The last modification is that each hour or at some other agreed upon time interval, the assets of all players are added up and the player with the most money and property automatically becomes the banker who wears a white hat if available.

What you will find when you play this game is that eventually one player will rule the board and must support all other players with loans from the bank. This supports the cycle of wealth that we observe in real life economic systems and the role of government in redistributing wealth to keep the peasants from revolting.

HAVE FUN!

ABOUT THE AUTHOR

Glenn A Metts lives in the US Virgin Islands having moved there in 2008. He is an entrepreneur, certified public accountant, professor, author, and sea captain. As an entrepreneur he started several businesses in such diverse fields as manufacturing, accounting and consulting, mechanical contracting, intellectual property, and commercial real estate. After semi-retiring he started teaching in the Purdue system and eventually moved on to the University of the Virgin Islands where he is an Associate Professor of Management and Director of Entrepreneurship Education. He has published academically in several journals and has presented papers at dozens of conferences in his field. He holds a USCG 100 ton Master Captain license and is an avid sailor, diver, adventurer, and general trouble-maker.

Made in the USA
Charleston, SC
07 December 2011